S0-BDM-171

Conversations with Colson Whitehead

Literary Conversations Series
Monika Gehlawat
General Editor

Books by Colson Whitehead

The Intuitionist. New York: Doubleday, 1999
John Henry Days. New York: Doubleday, 2001
The Colossus of New York: A City in Thirteen Parts. New York: Doubleday, 2003
Apex Hides the Hurt. New York: Doubleday, 2006
Sag Harbor. New York: Doubleday, 2009
Zone One. New York: Doubleday, 2011
The Noble Hustle: Poker, Beef Jerky, and Death. New York: Doubleday, 2014
The Underground Railroad. New York: Doubleday, 2016

Conversations with Colson Whitehead

Edited by Derek C. Maus

University Press of Mississippi / Jackson

The University Press of Mississippi is the scholarly publishing agency of
the Mississippi Institutions of Higher Learning: Alcorn State University,
Delta State University, Jackson State University, Mississippi State University,
Mississippi University for Women, Mississippi Valley State University,
University of Mississippi, and University of Southern Mississippi.

www.upress.state.ms.us

The University Press of Mississippi is a member
of the Association of University Presses.

First printing 2019
∞

Library of Congress Cataloging-in-Publication Data

Names: Whitehead, Colson, 1969–interviewee. | Maus, Derek C., editor.
Title: Conversations with Colson Whitehead / edited by Derek C. Maus.
Description: Jackson : University Press of Mississippi, [2019] |
Series: Literary Conversations Series | Includes index. |
Identifiers: LCCN 2018038411 (print) | LCCN 2018041319 (ebook) | ISBN
9781496821485 (epub single) | ISBN 9781496821492 (epub institutional) | ISBN
9781496821508 (pdf single) | ISBN 9781496821515 (pdf institutional) | ISBN
9781496821522 (hardback : alk. paper) | ISBN 9781496821478 (pbk. : alk. paper)
Subjects: LCSH: Whitehead, Colson, 1969-—Interviews. | Authors,
American—20th century—Interviews. | LCGFT: Interviews.
Classification: LCC PS3573.H4768 (ebook) | LCC PS3573.
H4768 Z46 2019 (print) | DDC 813/.54 [B]—dc23
LC record available at https://lccn.loc.gov/2018038411

British Library Cataloging-in-Publication Data available

Contents

Introduction

"No matter what you write, there's probably someone smarter and more talented than you who has written it before. All you can hope is that you have something to bring to the table, and that you have your distinct point of view to add."

Taking Colson Whitehead's public utterances purely at face value, one can be left with the impression that he doesn't believe that he leaves much of a mark on his world. The self-deprecating tone he frequently adopts in his interviews and his nonfictional writings regularly goes far beyond writerly humility in the degree to which it seems designed to paint a picture of an awkward hermit. For example, in the opening of his autobiographical *New Yorker* essay entitled "A Psychotronic Childhood," he remarks, "I was a bit of a shut-in. I would prefer to have been a sickly child . . . [b]ut the truth is that I just didn't like leaving the house."[1] Near the conclusion of that essay, he also directs what seem like harsh criticisms at himself in lamenting his early lack of success as a professional writer: "I'd tried to sell a novel before, one with a similarly ludicrous-sounding premise and had got dumped by my high-powered agent. Now here I was doing it again. Like an imbecile."[2] While visiting Harvard, his alma mater, in 2003, he tells a reporter from the student newspaper that he "turned his papers in late, sat in the back of his classes, and . . . didn't say anything"[3] during his four years in Cambridge. In a 2016 interview with Jesse McCarthy for the Harvard alumni magazine, he adds to this unprepossessing portrait of a young man as an undergraduate: "I considered myself a writer, but I didn't actually write anything. . . . I wore black and smoked cigarettes, but I didn't actually sit down and write, which apparently is part of the process of writing." Lest one think these are merely sardonic retrospectives on the foibles of his youth and early adulthood, Whitehead also produces a book-length exemplar of it in *The Noble Hustle: Poker, Beef Jerky, and Death,* an account of his participation in the 2011 World Series of Poker as a putative representative of the "Republic of Anhedonia" (the name of which is emblazoned on the jacket he wears in his author's photograph on the book's dust cover). The book's opening line—"I have a good poker face because I'm half dead inside"[4]—presages a litany of mordant comments such as "I'd long aspired to the laid-back lifestyle of exhibits at Madame Tussaud's. There are cool perks. You don't have to move around that much, or waste energy on fake smiles, and every now and then someone shows up to give you a good dusting."[5] Throughout the book, Whitehead walks the narrative tightrope of engaging the reader's interest and even sympathy while providing very little evidence to suggest that his self-diagnosed affliction—"the inability to experience pleasure"—is merely a literary conceit.

Although an earnest literary critic might be inclined to see Whitehead's self-fashioning as a *schlemiel* to be a kind of homage to Thomas Pynchon (whom Whitehead cites on numerous occasions as a germinal influence), I will suppress the desire to make such a claim and instead put forth the proposition that he doth protest a bit too much . . . albeit very much by design. To be clear, Whitehead's idiosyncratic set of pop-cultural interests undoubtedly made it desirable for him to retreat to the sanctity of "[lying] on the living-room carpet, watching horror movies."[6] It is likewise not difficult to imagine a teenaged Whitehead resembling Benji Cooper, the protagonist of his novel *Sag Harbor*, in struggling to explain his musical tastes to his peers, whether translating Grandmaster Flash to his predominantly white classmates at the posh Trinity School in Manhattan or justifying his penchant for early goth music to his African American friends during their shared Long Island summers. Benji informs the reader at one point, "Let's just put it out there: I liked the Smiths."[7] Such sheepish admissions surely discomforted both the novel's creator and its protagonist. In his 2009 interview with Marie Mockett, Whitehead even reduces himself to an autobiographical foil for Benji, his fictional nebbish: "I had a set of disorganized life experiences and needed to discover how to shape, spindle, and mutilate them into an interesting story. Drab piece of cheap bond manipulated into gorgeous origami crane, that's my motto."

Whether the flesh-and-blood Colson Whitehead is actually as much of a "drab piece of cheap bond" as he makes himself out to be is a matter best attested to by his friends and family, but I believe that the public self that he propagates through his interviews, his readings, his nonfiction, and his Twitter feed—@colsonwhitehead, if you're interested—is a meticulously curated construction that involves nearly as much forethought and clever execution as can be found in any of his novels. Far from being an accusation of insincerity or inauthenticity, this claim is intended as a fundamental premise in my attempt at unifying a written corpus that often seems designed by its inherent diversity of forms and themes to frustrate all efforts at cohesive interpretation. When asked about the variance within his work, Whitehead often repeats some version of what he tells Nikesh Shukla in a 2013 interview: "I think I just don't want to do the same thing over and over again, so on one level each book becomes an antidote to the one [that] came before." I believe that Whitehead consciously identifies what one might call his "peculiar ordinariness" as the source of his problems with fitting into society. He alludes to such a seemingly oxymoronic condition when he describes the traits that allow Mark Spitz, the protagonist of his novel *Zone One*, to survive in a world brought low by a zombie apocalypse: "If you're smart, you kill yourself. If you're dumb, you're not going to make it. That leaves the rest of us."[8] He directly cites his parents' adoption of "doomed product lines and hexed formats" such as the Betamax (instead of VHS), a TRS-80 home computer (instead of an Apple II), and Intellivision video-game system (instead of an Atari 1600) as having been "good training for a writer, for the sooner you accept the fact that you are a deluded idiot who is always out of step with reality the better off you will be."[9] He reframes his family's ill-starred participation in technological consumerism neither as principled iconoclasm nor as abject failure, but, rather as the metaphorical lemons from which he makes his literary lemonade. Despite its ample and demonstrable brilliance, Whitehead's writing seems less focused on celebrating exceptionality as the means for solving human problems than it is on discovering how to carve out a meaningful existence (and continue to make art) despite the daunting obstacles within individual people, social structures, literary traditions, and ultimately one's self.

The role that race plays both in Whitehead's self-conception and in his writing illustrates this point. Despite what some reviewers and critics have insisted, Whitehead is not a "postracial" writer. If his mocking 2009 *New York Times* op-ed piece entitled "The Year of Living Postracially" doesn't convey his disdain for this concept clearly enough, he also explicitly rejects it while speaking with Shukla four years later: "I think you're only postracial when you stop asking if you're postracial." Others (myself included) have attempted to apply other terms such as "post-soul" or "post-black" to Whitehead's authorial perspective, but Donovan X. Ramsey may have most trenchantly articulated the manner in which race signifies in the bulk of Whitehead's fiction: "*Sag Harbor* isn't postracial. It might be described as metaracial because, while race does have [its] place in the novel . . . it doesn't give race prominence over the everyday suckiness of being a teenager. It doesn't cheapen the experience [of] growing up by trying to turn Benji into Bigger Thomas. The pleasure of reading a book like *Sag Harbor* for a black man of similar circumstance is in its treatment of the young black male condition as human above anything else and the subsequent organic social commentary that sprouts up around that precious offering."[10]

What Ramsey calls *Sag Harbor*'s "metaracial" quality separates Whitehead from one of his earliest exemplary characters, the elevator scholar James Fulton. The manuscript of a mysterious and possibly illusory second volume of his book, *Theoretical Elevators*, becomes the focus of an obsessive search by nearly all characters in Whitehead's debut novel, *The Intuitionist*. It purports to describe a radical new form of elevator that will bring about an almost incomprehensible change in the conception of reality, on par with Copernican heliocentrism and Einsteinian relativity. Upon learning that Fulton is a black man passing as white, the novel's protagonist, Lila Mae Watson, makes the discovery and dissemination of his lost work her primary goal in life. As numerous critics have pointed out, she sees the "uplift" that the radically new elevator promises not simply in engineering terms but also racial ones, believing it to offer the cure to the rampant discrimination that she has faced as the only black female elevator inspector in the city. The partial discovery of the missing manuscript at the end of the novel fulfills neither of these lofty goals, thereby removing the possibility of interpreting Fulton as a messianic figure heralding a "second elevation."[11] However, it does indirectly provide Lila Mae with a new and seemingly more purposeful existence than the one offered by continuing to toil for the corrupt bureaucracy that constrains her at every turn; at the end of the novel, she devotes herself to completing Fulton's work on the "Black Box," a project whose ultimate feasibility remains indeterminate. The resolution of Lila Mae's story in no way cancels out the significance—positive or negative—of her (or Fulton's) blackness, but for the time being it becomes secondary to her elemental humanization via the act of writing.

Since his earliest interviews, Whitehead has treated his own racial identity in ways that complicate its ability to pigeonhole him. In his first published interview (unfortunately not included in this volume), Whitehead tells Laura Miller of *Salon.com* in 1999 that he felt himself to be part of a new generation of African American writers who were empowered to break through the limitations faced by black writers from earlier generations: "Now I think there are a lot more of us writing and a lot more different areas we're exploring. It's not as polemicized. I'm dealing with serious race issues, but I'm not handling them in a way that people expect."[12] In a similar vein, when Walter Mosley asks him during their 2001 interview about his reaction to being identified explicitly as a black writer, Whiteheads responds that "[i]t's like the 'N' word. It depends who's saying it. I feel like I'm trying to face black literature, I'm trying to extend the canon of black literature, and I'm a black writer doing this." Eight years and three books further into his publishing career, Whitehead amends this statement slightly, telling Rob Spillman in 2009,

> When I was starting off I was very essentialist—I'm a black writer. I was very self-conscious about what a black writer was. Like, I wasn't going to write about a shack in the South, walking down the road with your messed-up shoes. There are certain clichés about black literature that I rebelled against . . . [Now] I feel like I'm just a writer trying to figure out the next book. While I did identify myself as a black writer at the beginning of my "career," I think that was a holdover from growing up in the seventies with the nationalist idea of what my role was. I'm fine with whatever the first line of review says, i.e., "black writer," "African American writer."

He is not specifically addressing race when he tells Melissa Locker in a 2011 interview that "nostalgia is one of my signs of creeping zombie-ism." However, when viewed in conjunction with his earlier comments, the distaste such a comment directs at "[b]eing stuck in particular grooves, unable to escape them" and at "[r]obotic devotion to the past" can reasonably be interpreted as a rejection of externally imposed expectations about how he should write. By 2016, Whitehead circles back explicitly to the authorial identity he adopted in his first interview, telling Boris Kachka that his comparative autonomy as a writer—and specifically as an African American writer—is a generational privilege that he welcomes: "I started writing in the '90s, so I was free to just have an eccentric career and not conform to some idea of what a black writer has to do. I didn't have the burden of representation. Growing up as a product of the black civil rights movement, I had a lot of different models for black weirdness, whether it's Richard Pryor or James Baldwin or Jimmy Walker." Again, without rendering it irrelevant or pretending it is not real, Whitehead embeds any significance attributable to his blackness within an overarching "weirdness" that frees him to write about race—and everything else—however he sees fit, a privilege that is extended automatically to writers who are not automatically identified by their race (a point he makes when he rhetorically asks Spillman, "Do people still say, 'Philip Roth, Jewish American writer?'"). By becoming "ordinary" in regard to the ostensible significance of his race, Whitehead feels at liberty to let his freak flag fly.

A comment that Whitehead makes while speaking with Linda Selzer in 2008 shows how his definition of literary "black weirdness" is premised on the varied influences that shaped his craft as a writer: "I don't see a distinction between the use of fantasy in, say, horror novels, and the use of fantastic elements in magical realism, the absurdity of Beckett, the surrealism of *Invisible Man.* The tweaked reality is a tool, and whether you use it for a 'low culture' purpose or a 'high culture' purpose is up to you." Although his audience may project particular value judgments onto his penchant for George Romero's zombie films or his allusions to Ellison and Pynchon, Whitehead apparently feels little obligation to alter his writing to meet such expectations. In fact, he seems inclined to frustrate (or, more accurately, to "weird") the expectations created in his readers by their recognition of familiar elements. As he tells Robbie Baden in 2010, "I think there are clichés when talking about race, and I want to avoid them. . . . I just think I'm a writer, and I have my own perspective that I'm putting out there. And I don't have to follow someone else's idea of how you write a novel or how you approach a subject. I'm hoping that people will come to my books assuming that I am doing something different." Such an assumption can be liberating when it works, but it can also push him to the margins when it doesn't. In my mind, the unconscionably scant recognition that *John Henry Days* and *Apex Hides the Hurt* have received among both critical and popular audiences is due to their idiosyncrasies not being accommodated in the way that they were for *The Underground Railroad.*

In a 2009 interview with Jeremiah Chamberlin, Whitehead introduces a tonal dimension to the "weirdness" that appears in his work by specifying a dissonance that he admired during his formative period: "Whether it's Beckett or Richard Pryor, artists who I liked growing up veer between the capricious horribleness of the everyday and the absurd beauty of existence. So for me the duality has always been important in terms of how I see the world, and I think that plays out in my fiction." As he revealed to Noah Charney in a 2016 interview, this duality is the root of his darkly satirical commentary on human nature in *Zone One*: "I can't say why it appeals to other people, but for me the act of transformation of a loved one, a friend or family member or neighbor . . . into the monster they've always been but kept hidden from you is very profound." Similarly, he tells Hilary Leichter in 2016 that he strove to create a narrator for *The Underground Railroad* who could "integrate some of the absurd, but also the truthful elements of [the protagonist's] world."

Given the dark subjects and uncertain endings of many of Whitehead's books, it is tempting to believe that he skews towards the "capricious horribleness" end of the dichotomy he describes to Chamberlin. The zombie hordes breaching the barriers erected by Mark Spitz and the other human survivors at the end of *Zone One* do not inspire great confidence in the prospects for reclaiming and restoring Manhattan, after all. Nevertheless, the fates of his two female protagonists—Lila Mae from *The Intuitionist* and Cora from *The Underground Railroad*—are emblematic of the at-times seemingly reluctant optimism that recurs throughout Whitehead's books. Whitehead frequently expresses a bleak view of humanity in his interviews and essays—e.g., "an artist is a monster that thinks it is human."[13] It may therefore seem counterintuitive to ascribe even a measured degree of hopefulness to him. Although Whitehead often flippantly locates the origins of the comic-satiric tenor of his work outside himself—as he does in telling Alyssa Rosenberg in 2011 that "I've always been much more grim and the jokes start seeping in"—it also bears repeating that satire is an inherently idealistic mode of expression; one *must* have some measure of hope about to want to reform someone/something via satire's mocking moral/ethical leverage, rather than simply to excoriate them with a harsher rhetorical mode such as invective. Especially in the interviews that followed in the wake of *The Underground Railroad*, Whitehead readily admits that becoming a parent (he has a daughter from his first marriage and a son from his second) has allowed him to accept a modestly rosier outlook. For example, he tells Vicky Mochama in 2016,

I think things improve and progress quite slowly. Certainly, I never thought we'd have a black president. For most of my life, that seemed inconceivable. . . . I have two kids who don't think it's odd at all that we have a black male president and a female candidate, so that is obviously an advancement. I can vote, I can publish; obviously, I'm not living under the yoke of slavery. Things improve slowly—not fast enough, because old systems die hard, but I certainly have the hope that my children and their generation are moving into a better world. Cora, when she takes that first fateful step off the plantation, believes that there's a better world out there. If you don't have hope, then why go on?

In speaking with Donna Seaman at roughly the same time, he echoes the sentiment of this final question in a way that sheds light not only on Cora's tenacity but also on how and why readers might be justified in seeing more hope—improbable or impossible though it may be—in the ambiguous endings of his earlier novels:

> The way I see it, one of the backbones of postapocalypse literature is the search for a safe refuge, whether in postnuclear war fiction or zombie novels. People are always looking for that human refuge over the next hill. Then they find a place and it's overrun, and they have to keep going. They're animated by a very improbable hope that they can be safe. I think that is what animates Mark Spitz in *Zone One* and a lot of heroes in postapocalypse literature. I think that impossible hope also animates Cora. Why should she believe that there is any place of freedom when all she's witnessed her whole life is the brutality of the plantation? Yet she persists.

Such persistence—despite the absence of reassurance or refuge—provides a means of interpreting the nonresolution of Lila Mae's story in *The Intuitionist* or Benji's barely perceptible steps towards maturity during the summer that passes in the course of *Sag Harbor* in positive, even expectant, terms. It also presents a parallel to Whitehead's strategies for surviving as both a nerdy child and an anhedonistic adult.

At the outset of his interview with Whitehead, McCarthy observes that "It's clear he does not enjoy talking about himself. He has always been highly skeptical of confessional modes." Similar comments can be found scattered throughout the increasingly frequent interviews that Whitehead has given, or perhaps been obliged to give, as his literary celebrity has grown incrementally. Although his reluctance to give interviews about his work does not approach that of such famously publicity-averse authors as Pynchon or Alice Munro, it becomes especially apparent in the interviews he has given in recent years that Whitehead has become quite efficient at delivering the verbal equivalent of a website's F.A.Q. section when he feels it appropriate. In fact, when I had the fortune of hearing him give a lecture about and reading from *The Underground Railroad* in Syracuse, New York, in September of 2017, I caught myself finishing some of his sentences as he delivered them to the audience in the hall, having read many of his anecdotes and punch lines previously while performing the research for this book. Of course, there is no shame in developing a shtick to handle the mind-numbing grind and innate repetitiveness of a publicity tour as extensive and protracted as the one Whitehead undertook for his massively successful novel. However, when considered in tandem with Whitehead's (largely) tongue-in-cheek misanthropy, McCarthy's comments about the author's discomfort with self-promotion and his "skeptic[ism] of confessional modes" invite the presumption that such formulaic interview answers are akin to the notorious nonanswers of professional football coach Bill Belichick, who memorably dismissed a series of questions by reporters during a press conference after a loss by simply repeating the phrase "We're on to Cincinnati" until the exasperated reporters gave up trying to elicit a substantive response.

But Whitehead is no Belichick (nor was he meant to be), at least not by inclination. His earliest interviews reveal a personality that is much less impinged upon by literary celebrity (and perhaps also by the more concrete demands of being a husband and father). Although his first two books, *The Intuitionist* and *John Henry Days*, were both critical successes, they did not thrust Whitehead into the popular spotlight as his later novels—*Sag Harbor*, *Zone One*, and *The Underground Railroad*—have done. When he sits down over lunch with Mosley in 2001, the two men range freely and warmly through a host of topics including literary influence, the complexities of the literary life, comic books, and more. Significantly, Whitehead uses his oft-maligned adolescent self in this interview to frame his iconoclastic literary aims: "I feel like my ideal reader is me at sixteen, or someone like me, who has just been reading the usual high school stuff and hasn't been exposed to some kind of freaky postwar black literature." Rather than marking himself as an uninviting "shut-in," Whitehead instead identifies his teenage avatar as "ideal" precisely *because* of his receptiveness to and even hunger for "freaky" literature, particularly the "black weirdness" that Whitehead seeks to express.

But such wholeheartedly devotion to "weirdness" is not without its hazards, a fact Whitehead seems to have known quite early in life. Even while breathlessly recounting the joys of an adolescence spent consuming splatter-flicks, he reminds his audience of the social side-effects of such geeky proclivities: "The clever reader will have caught on that I was not dating much. I was on my own."[14] He revisits this theme in a 2009 interview with Corban Goble, noting that the praise (or condemnation) of critics does nothing to alter the fundamental isolation of the writerly life: "A good review is a good review and a bad review is a bad review. No matter what kind of reviews you get each day, the problem is the same. How do you create art? You can get some nice kudos or some condemnation, but the blank page is always waiting for you the next day. You're always alone the next day no matter how many things people said about you the day before." In a similar vein, Whitehead tells Stephenie Harrison in their 2016 interview that the relative inconspicuousness he experienced at the outset of his career can be partly attributed to his initial tendency to write stories with presumably small readerships: "[W]hen you're writing about elevator inspectors, you don't necessarily think you're going to have a lot of mass appeal. I've always loved giving my weird takes on the world and writing books that sound a little oddball and maybe even turn some people off." Throughout his career, Whitehead shows himself to be keenly aware of both the influences that have shaped his development as a writer and of his desire to transcend (or at least to complicate) those influences in his literary creations. He also recognizes the manner in which this desire runs contrary to many readers' tastes and expectations when choosing works of literature. It is precisely these forms of self-consciousness that allow for—or perhaps even necessitate—his cultivation of an outsider's persona as his career develops. Whitehead's embrace of what he calls "tweaked reality" in his interview with Selzer requires detachment from convention, whether social or literary.

The outlines of this detachment are already visible in the handful of interviews he conducted after the publication of *John Henry Days*. In a 2006 interview with "Dave" from *Powells.com*, Whitehead notes that his attitude towards John Henry shifted dramatically while writing about him: "I always liked him. I first heard about him as a kid, and there weren't a lot of black superheroes growing up. Marvel Comics had their Falcon and Luke Cage, but the story always struck a chord with me . . . [A]s I did more research, I started to recall the central ambiguity of the story, which I think is why I gravitated toward it. Different characters espouse their point of view, whether or not it was a triumph of the individual. For me, I still have no idea what the hell the John Henry story means, even now." Similarly, in discussing the indeterminate temporal and geographic setting of *The Intuitionist* with Matthew Sharpe in 2003, Whitehead makes it clear that the ambiguity he builds into this aspect of the book is both intentional and intrinsic not only to his artistic goals but also to the book's connection to his own time and place: "I think there's an interesting tension when you can't pin it down, and there are these different kinds of inputs that are telling you one thing on one page and another thing on another page. I think that that confusion mimics racial confusion at large in the country. Has Civil Rights happened or has it not happened? You can read the newspaper and feel that same confusion." Whether he frames his intentions as sowing ambiguity or confusion, Whitehead leaves no doubt that his reader should abandon all hope that his books will provide them with a reassuringly familiar resolution.

Whitehead's comments in interviews often express his profound distrust of received truths, the ultimate source of most such tidy endings. As he tells Sherman, "I don't find history very reliable; there's a white history, and there's a black history. And I grew up at a time in college and right after college when there was this crazy deconstructionist sort of thing that nothing exists, everything is fluid, meaning in itself is fluid. It's hard to keep up with everyone's version of the truth; they cancel each other out." More than a decade later in 2012, he tells Nancy Smith that even though he writes "the books that I'm compelled to," he does not believe that this sense of compulsion transfers a corresponding didacticism into his work: "I definitely learn things about the world when I write them, and I hope that other people get something out of them, enjoy them, see the world differently when they're done. I can't say that you should extract this or that value from my books explicitly. They are up for interpretation." One consistently gets the sense that Whitehead feels enlivened by the process of exploring difficult questions, even or especially when he knows that no definitive answers are forthcoming. As noted above, it is the persistence in the face of such a situation that he values, much as Richard Wright concludes his memoir *Black Boy* by resolving to "hurl words into the darkness and wait for an echo . . . to keep alive in our hearts a sense of the inexpressibly human."[15]

In 2002 while working on the collection of impressionistic essays that eventually coalesced into *The Colossus of New York*, Whitehead tells Evette Porter, "I think I identify myself with the metropolis. But America is bigger than the seven-mile strip of Manhattan. So partially, I'm trying to figure out how I fit into America through these different people." One may balk at trying to square this quasi-Whitmanesque effort to "contain multitudes" with the benumbed tone of *The Noble Hustle*, but I would argue they are far more similar than meets the eye. Even *The Noble Hustle*'s comparatively dire version of Whitehead-as-narrator/protagonist manages to find his kith and kin as he drifts among the poker tables of Las Vegas in a low-grade postdivorce depression. Tellingly, he identifies them using a series of terms he has directed at himself in various venues through the years:

> I was gonna play in the Big Game and give it my best shot. It was not the National Series of Poker, it was the World Series of Poker, and I would represent my country, the Republic of Anhedonia. We have no borders, but the population teems. No one has deigned to write our history, but we are an ancient land, founded during the original disappointments, when the first person met another person. I would do it for my countrymen, the shut-ins, the doom-struck, the morbid of temperament, for all those who walk through life with poker faces 24/7 because they never learned any other way.[16]

Throughout his career, Whitehead's attempts at trying to figure out how he and/or his characters fit into America never reaches anything approaching a conventional conclusion. Even the materially privileged Benji from *Sag Harbor* feels trapped by a distinctly bourgie brand of DuBoisian double consciousness that arises from being one of the "black boys with beach houses" who spend their summers in the town whose name the novel bears: "According to the world we were the definition of paradox: black boys with beach houses. A paradox to the outside, but it never occurred to us that there was anything strange about it. It was simply who we were." Although Benji tries to assert his distance from this external imposition of strangeness with another echo of Whitman—"What you call paradox, I call *myself*"—he also adds that "[t]hose inclined to this remedy didn't have many obvious models."[17]

This latter passage helps explain Whitehead's recurrent self-identification as an introverted eccentric. Neither the nerdy Benji nor the prickly Lila Mae are ever going to find the process of finding a meaningful place for themselves easy, given not only the fundamental barriers against belonging that they face in the respective Americas that they inhabit, but also the conflicting (at best) or damaging (at worst) counsel they receive from prospective mentors—i.e., models—for how to survive. Benji—solidifying his linkages back to the real-life Whitehead of "A Psychotronic Childhood"—reveals his dilemma early on in *Sag Harbor*:

> I was one of those dullards who thought that "Just be yourself" was the wisdom of the ages, the most calming piece of advice I had ever heard, and acted accordingly. It enabled these words, for example, to escape my mouth: "I can't wait for Master of Horror George A. Romero to make another film. *Fangoria* magazine—still the best horror and sci-fi magazine around if you ask me—says he has trouble raising funding, but I think Hollywood is just scared of what he has to say." . . . Statements (of simple truth!) that had been harmless weeks ago were now symptoms of disease. And possibly catching. I was just being myself, and I was just being avoided. For whole, contaminated semesters now.[18]

Such relatively mild difficulties are greatly magnified in both the postapocalyptic, zombie-haunted landscape that Mark Spitz inhabits in *Zone One* and in the series of equally dehumanizing (if differently constituted) states through which Cora passes in her attempts to escape from slavery in *The Underground Railroad*. The protagonists of *John Henry Days* and *Apex Hides the Hurt* both demonstrate the undesirability and ineffectiveness of trying to find a place for oneself by "selling out," though neither novel prescribes a solution to the problems that led them to such a stratagem in the first place.

What all of these characters have in common with each other (and seemingly also with their creator) is that they will assuredly *not* succeed in finding a place by doing what is expected of them; neither are they guaranteed any comfort solely from their refusal to conform. In his interview with Sherman, Whitehead notes he found it undesirable to cast John Henry as a clear-cut conquering hero in retelling his story: "The John Henry myth is so ambiguous. He challenges the mechanical steam drill that will replace him to a race; he drills faster and farther and wins, and then he dies from the exertion. So is that a triumph? Is it a defeat? Is it a triumph for the individual, a triumph for the machine, a necessary sacrifice that the community needs? I was trying to emphasize that kind of ambiguity." Given that Whitehead tells Selzer that he deems Beckett's famously unresolved play *Waiting for Godot* to be a work of high realism, it is unsurprising that he would be more comfortable with frustrated resolutions than the average person. He embraces the validity of misfits (like himself) without ever overstating their ability to change either themselves or their world for the better. John Henry may have won his race with the steam drill, but he also perishes as a result of it. Whitehead has a more tempered hope for the efficacy of his own figurative hammer-swings: "To fully inhabit one's delusions, to give in to every kooky aspect of one's freakishness—it's a handy survival strategy."[19]

Acknowledgments

I would like to express my gratitude to a number of individuals who assisted me greatly during the year-long process of assembling this volume. For their direct and material forms of assistance in such tasks as locating copies of individual interviews and/or securing the rights to those interviews I wish to offer my gratitude not only to all of the original authors of those interviews, but also to Brooke Barona, Lora Evinger, Adrienne Ingrum, Amy Swauger, Jill Owens Leigh, Shannon McCullough, Maud Newton, Cheston Knapp, Joy Priest, Elise Blackwell, Ashley Strosnider, Gerti Wilson, Silvia Killingsworth, Marisa Siegel, Katie Rowland, Lynn Green, David Bressler, Halimah Marcus, Jean Martin, Alex Posey, Jordan Ginsberg, Jared Bland, Jen Singerman, Keir Graff, and Bill Ott.

I would also like to thank all the employees of Crumb Library, especially those responsible for handling my occasionally obscure interlibrary loan requests with great aplomb and efficiency. It is never easy getting the research materials you need when you live and work far off the beaten path (literally and figuratively), but the librarians with whom I work have never once failed me and for that I am deeply indebted.

For other forms of personal and/or professional support, I would like to thank the following colleagues. Without their mindful and conscientious examples, I might long ago have abandoned my willingness to slog through the dismal swamp of academic bureaucracy for the payoff of being able to talk and to write about literature for a living on a daily basis: Bertram D. Ashe, John Bailyn, Trevor Blank, M. Keith Booker, Kimberly Bouchard, Owen E. Brady, Darryl Dickson-Carr, James J. Donahue, Christine Doran, Petra Eckhard, David Fregoe, Polly Gannon, Walter Hölbling, Dijana Jelača, Katarzyna Jerzak, Maurice Kenny, Serj Kirchano, Luvena Kopp, Rebecca Lehmann, Madeline Levine, Jo Luloff, Donald J. McNutt, Anna Neva, Susan Novak, Tanja Petrović, Tim Portice, Christopher Putney, Masha Sokolova, Alan Steinberg, Anthony Stewart, Anna Surovegina, Terry Tiernan, Janet Tucker, William Tucker, Julia Vashtalova, Mitja Velikonja, Eileen Visser, Linda Wagner-Martin, Katharina Wiedlack, and John Youngblood.

I would like to thank Richard Page Wright for having the foresight to give me a copy (signed, no less!) of *The Intuitionist* as a gift way back in 2000, when I knew nothing about the book or its author. I am deeply sorry we lost touch over the years, my friend, but I am also eternally grateful that you knew me well enough to put that book in my hands.

I would like to thank my wife, Stephanie Tritt, for her love and her friendship (and for also being a fan of Whitehead's books from the second she read the first line of *Zone One* . . .). I cannot think of anyone else with whom I would want to drive five hours on a school night to hear Whitehead talk about his work.

I would like to thank Oscar Tritt Maus for waiting until nearly all of the editing for this book was done before he arrived in this world. Your father promises to do his best to resist the temptation to read *Zone One* to you as a bedtime story (maybe *Apex Hides the Hurt*?).

I would like to thank my parents, Anneliese and Warren Maus, for setting the reading hook in me early on and filling their houses with books so that I always had something to read nearby, even when the siren-song of television was insistently playing.

Finally, I would like to thank Figgy, Frances, Gogol, and Yoko for all the mind-clearing walks in the woods, the affectionately insistent bumps of cold and wet noses in the early morning hours, and the steadfast companionship that human beings would be wise to emulate more often. It's a shame y'all can't read, though . . .

DCM

Notes

1. Colson Whitehead, "A Psychotronic Childhood: Learning from B-Movies," *New Yorker* 88.16 (4 Jun. 2012), 98.

2. Whitehead, "A Psychotronic Childhood," 105.

3. Sanders I. Bernstein, "Colson Whitehead '91: One of Harvard's Recent Authors Keeps It Real," *thecrimson.com* (16 Apr. 2009).

4. Colson Whitehead, *The Noble Hustle: Poker, Beef Jerky, and Death* (New York: Doubleday, 2014), 3.

5. Whitehead, *The Noble Hustle*, 80.

6. Whitehead, "A Psychotronic Childhood," 98.

7. Colson Whitehead, *Sag Harbor* (New York: Doubleday, 2009), 63.

8. Alexis Madrigal, "Bookforum Talks with Colson Whitehead," *bookforum.com* (17 Oct. 2011).

9. Whitehead, "A Psychotronic Childhood," 100.

10. Donovan X. Ramsey, "Coming of Age in Sag Harbor," *donovanxramsey.com* (27 Dec. 2010).

11. Colson Whitehead, *The Intuitionist* (New York: Doubleday, 1999), 134.

12. Laura Miller, "Going Up," *salon.com* (12 Jan. 1999).

13. Whitehead, "A Psychotronic Childhood," 104.

14. Whitehead, "A Psychotronic Childhood," 103.

15. Richard Wright, *Black Boy* (New York: HarperCollins, 1945), 135.

16. Whitehead, *The Noble Hustle*, 20.

17. Whitehead, *Sag Harbor*, 57, 58.

18. Whitehead, *Sag Harbor*, 23–24.

19. Whitehead, "A Psychotronic Childhood," 105.

Chronology

1969	Born on November 6 in New York to Arch S. Whitehead III and Mary Ann Woody Whitehead.
1987	Graduates from Trinity School in Manhattan, New York. Leaves in the fall to attend Harvard University in Cambridge, Massachusetts.
1987–1991	Attends Harvard University, earning a BA in English literature.
1991	Returns to New York.
1991–1996	Writes about television, music, books, and culture for *The Village Voice*.
1996	Begins writing the novel that eventually becomes *The Intuitionist*.
1997–1998	Lives in San Francisco and works as a copywriter for an Internet start-up company.
1998	Returns to New York.
1999	Publishes *The Intuitionist*.
2000	Receives the Whiting Award for Fiction. Receives the Quality Paperback Book Club's New Voices Award for *The Intuitionist*.
2001	Publishes *John Henry Days*.
2002	Receives MacArthur Fellowship. Receives the Anisfield-Wolf Book Award and the New York Public Library's Young Lions Fiction Award for *John Henry Days*.
2003	Publishes *The Colossus of New York: A City in Thirteen Parts*.
2006	Publishes *Apex Hides the Hurt*.
2007	Receives fellowship at the New York Public Library's Dorothy and Lewis B. Cullman Center for Scholars and Writers.
2008	Receives the PEN Oakland/Josephine Miles Literary Award for *Apex Hides the Hurt*.

2009   Publishes *Sag Harbor*. Begins posting on his @colsonwhitehead Twitter account on March 15.

2011   Publishes *Zone One*. Plays in and reports on the World Series of Poker for the *Grantland.com* website.

2012   Receives the Dos Passos Prize from Longwood University. Reports on the London Summer Olympic Games for *Grantland.com*.

2013   Receives Guggenheim Fellowship for Creative Arts.

2014   Publishes *The Noble Hustle: Poker, Beef Jerky, and Death.*

2016   Publishes *The Underground Railroad*, which earns him the National Book Award for Fiction.

2017   Receives the Carnegie Medal for Excellence in Fiction, the Pulitzer Prize for Fiction, and the Arthur C. Clarke Award for *The Underground Railroad*.

2018   Receives the Harvard Arts Medal recognizing artistic achievement by a Harvard University alumnus/alumna.

Conversations with Colson
Whitehead

Eavesdropping

Walter Mosley / 2001

From *Book* (May 2001): 44–47. Reprinted with permission from Barnes & Noble Booksellers, Inc. Barnes & Noble and the Barnes & Noble logo are trademarks owned and/or controlled by Barnes & Noble Booksellers, Inc., or its affiliates. All rights reserved.

Lured by the dual promises of a midday meal at a famous Brooklyn eatery and the opportunity to meet an admired colleague, Colson Whitehead and Walter Mosley accepted an invitation from *Book* to dine at Junior's Restaurant a couple of months before Whitehead's second novel, *John Henry Days*, a rumination on the legendary black folk hero, was released.

Walter Mosley, forty-nine, the award-winning author of six Easy Rawlins mysteries and a half dozen other books, arrives punctually and hangs up his fedora and overcoat before sitting down. Whitehead—whose debut, *The Intuitionist*, was a critically acclaimed genre-bending novel about an elevator inspector-cum-detective working in a retro future in an unnamed New York—walks in a little after 1 p.m., having recently awoken. "You know what you're having?" Mosley asks. "A salad," Whitehead says, which elicits a "Damn" from Mosley before he orders ribs, fried chicken, a cup of matzo ball soup, and three small Perriers. This is their first meeting, though the two have been paying attention to each other for years. Mosley made a strong impression with his first book, 1990's *Devil in a Blue Dress*, and hasn't let up since as a novelist, essayist, critic, or filmmaker; besides Easy Rawlins, the reluctant detective who was played by Denzel Washington in the 1995 screen adaptation, he's also written a series of stories starring Socrates Fortlow. His new lead character, Fearless Jones, appears in June. Whitehead, thirty-one, was hailed as a next big thing by critics, reviewers, and blurb artists—including Mosley—when *The Intuitionist* was published two years ago; *Fearless Jones* has been eagerly anticipated. The two shared opinions on topics ranging from Ralph Ellison to Spider-Man. And Gina Gershon got name-checked as well.

Mosley: Why is John Henry important to you?
Whitehead: I guess I just always really dug him, in elementary school.

Mosley: Me too.
Whitehead: And just as a kid, he was the first black superhero I knew. I grew up in the early seventies, and one day—I think it was third or fourth grade—the teacher said, "We're going to see a movie," and it was a half-hour cartoon about John Henry. It was really moving. It was a black family in a cartoon; they were dynamic. John Henry is a superhero, and he's fighting a machine.

Mosley: How did you feel about him losing to that machine? Because that made me cry.
Whitehead: I didn't cry.

Mosley: I was so upset.
Whitehead: I didn't know what to make of it, which is why I guess I had to write about it later on, because does he win or not? Does the machine win? Or, do the dehumanizing forces win? Is he affirmed, or is it a useless gesture?

Mosley: So now, many years later, what's your answer?
Whitehead: I still don't think I know.

Mosley: I guess I don't either. But I always felt bad about it. But he did win, right?
Whitehead: He actually wins the race, yeah.

Mosley: Then he dies. A blood vessel breaks in his head.
Whitehead: Yeah, so I think a lot of *John Henry Days* is about how do we interpret that? The book jumps around in different decades, different people: a blues man in the thirties, a sheet music writer in the 1910s, sort of struggling against their own personal machines. Can we win? What does winning mean? So I think it will provide a lot of different answers. You can walk away thinking, "Yeah, John Henry wins," or "No, John Henry loses," and it would be okay with the book.

Mosley: One of the things I like about your work is that I don't really feel like you're trying to tell me what to think.

Whitehead: I think you can read a book when you're ten, twenty and thirty, and fifty and sixty, and have different interpretations of that book. And that's what's great about art.

On Being a Black Writer

Mosley: If somebody says, "Colson Whitehead, the black writer," what do you think about that?

Whitehead: I always thought it was great. When I was in college and I was trying to find what I couldn't find in course classes, in the black section, there're all the people you heard about that you were supposed to read. There are all sorts of interpretations you can put on being a *black* writer. Are you not being put in the same category as white writers?

Mosley: It is an interesting question. The other night I went to Toni Morrison's seventieth birthday party. It was a big thing, five hundred people. Rita Dove and I were the emcees of it. Everybody was there. Now somebody got up there and had to give a speech and, in this speech, said Toni Morrison is the first black writer—no, first black woman writer—to be awarded the Nobel Prize. This person went on to say she was the first black and the first black woman to do a series of other things, and I didn't like it. I didn't want to hear it, and I didn't want to hear someone talk about Toni like that. Damn. She wins the fucking Nobel Prize, and I still have to say, "Well, you know, but she's a black woman"? Come on. Really. At some point or another you have to say, "Damn." I'm looking at *The Intuitionist*, and I would say this is a major literary event in American letters. I wish to claim you as a black writer on some levels, but on other levels, I don't want to. And really, I don't mind. When people say, "Walter Mosley, the black writer," this is fine; I don't mind. I don't care. You know, I am a black mystery writer, I'm a black blah-blah writer, or whatever kind of black writer I am, it's all right. But on some levels, I get upset. And I especially get upset for other people, not so much for myself.

Whitehead: It's like the "N" word. It depends who's saying it. I feel like I'm trying to face black literature, I'm trying to extend the canon of black literature, and I'm a black writer doing this.

Mosley: Who do you see as your audience?

Whitehead: The people who show up really change from venue to venue. When it first came out and people hadn't read the book and they heard it was crazy elevator inspectors, I got a lot of sci-fi and comic book fans. Then when I read last week, it was mostly middle-aged women who had book clubs.

Mosley: Did you lose that original audience?

Whitehead: No, I think they'll be back for the reading at the hipster book-store. I'm always surprised at the faces who show up and just grateful that there is an audience, to tell you the truth.

Mosley: Anybody. I don't care who you are, just come. That's really true about being a writer. "Aren't you upset that there are only white people in the audience?" No. They were buying books, and I was very happy to see them.

Whitehead: I feel like my ideal reader is me at sixteen, or someone like me, who has just been reading the usual high school stuff and hasn't been exposed to some kind of freaky postwar black literature—when I was six-teen, I was reading Stephen King. . . . Last week I did a thing for this Writers in Schools program in DC. The teacher had taught the book two days before, and I went in and talked about the book. And the kids were incredibly smart and thoughtful. They seemed to get the book. They didn't ask the same sort of questions I usually get. . . . They see me as the novelist guy, which I still have a hard time seeing myself as. I guess I am a novelist, but they see me as a Novelist with a capital "N."

Mosley: You do well not to see yourself—or anyone else—in that way because all of a sudden you start to sound like a baritone. [Deep voice] "Well, you know, I was thinking just the other day . . ." [normal voice] and that's just awful.

On Movies, Comics and Agents Who Quit

Mosley: Have you done any writing of screenplays?

Whitehead: Ten years ago I had this crazy thing. I was in college, and I wrote a script for this small production company. It was the most horrible experience.

Mosley: Did they pay you?

Whitehead: Yeah—very little. Meanwhile, it's this *Risky Business* meets *House Party*, some sort of black teen genre thing. It was so ridiculous and dumb. I'd get these notes: "How 'bout the main character gets in jail and has to rap his way out of being attacked by other prisoners." Aaaah, I signed a contract, and I'm totally debasing myself.

Mosley: It's really true, though. It's the same as writing articles for a magazine. It's not so much beforehand they tell you what to write—it's after you've written it; they start cutting things out. . . . Films—what are you thinking?

Whitehead: When the elevator inspector book came out, I got a lot of calls from big-name people who were like, "We love the book," and we'd have lunch. Then they'd read the last fifty pages and realize there isn't a big car crash at the end of the book, and I wouldn't hear from them again. They'd also realize that the main character is a black woman, and we can't get funding for a black woman detective.

Mosley: Can we make her a man?
Whitehead: Yeah, or make her Gina Gershon or–

Mosley: —Jennifer Tilly, hey. Shit. That's a movie right there. She could be black. You know, Larry Block had a character, the Burglar, I forgot his name, but they made the movie. It's a white, Jewish guy who's a burglar, and they made it Whoopi Goldberg. So it's a black woman with a Jewish name—that's close—which I think was kind of wonderful. But that's what happens.
Whitehead: I have a cousin I'm very close to, and he's a young filmmaker. Last summer he says, "Let's make some crazy action movie we always wanted to make when we were kids after reading comics and watching *Alien* and *Road Warrior* ten times in a row." We're working on it on and off. We'll see what happens. You know, it's fun making it up; it's fun to have the kind of rapport where you can say, "Let's rip off *Spider-Man 178* where Electro does this," and the other person knows what you're saying.

Mosley: You read Marvel [Comics]?
Whitehead: I was a Marvel guy, yeah.

Mosley: I have this gigantic collection, it's like thirty thousand, and I've been lately accruing the first hundred *Fantastic Four*s. I have no end of love for it, no end of love.
Whitehead: A couple years ago my parents were cleaning out a storage space that we had and they said, "Come get your stuff." And I was like, "I don't have any stuff in there." My brother shows up one day with about ten

boxes of comic books I hadn't seen in years, so I read half of them over again. It was such fun, such kicks.

Mosley: It's still kind of wonderful for adolescent boys, and also for young black men—the whole notion of a need to become so much more than you are in order to just get what a normal everyday person gets. I have to be Spider-Man. I have to be the Thing. I have to be as smart as Reed Richards. I can't just be a normal person and go to school and get out and expect shit, because nobody has anything. I think for young black men there's also a desire to go further than yourself: I can jump up on top of that building and swing from place to place, and if somebody came up behind me, I could sense it. You can never sneak up on me. I can tell danger. The whole idea—I find it really interesting. . . . So you're working on your third novel? And you're a novelist, but not with a capital "N"—
Whitehead: No, not yet.

Mosley: —But, you'd be dead if you have a capital "N" in your name. Is there anything other than that that you want to do?
Whitehead: I'm really digging this lifestyle. It's been a strange five years from when I first sent the [first] book out to people. No one liked it. Then my agent actually dumped me.

Mosley: Really?
Whitehead: Yeah. So I had to start over again from scratch when I finished *The Intuitionist.* I sent it [the first book] out to about twenty-five publishers. No one really liked it. After six months I got a call from my agent, and she's like, "Later for you."

Mosley: We want tunas that taste good, not tunas with good taste. That must have been really depressing.
Whitehead: It was, because you have all these rejection letters and the person who you thought was your one ally is like, "So where do we send these manuscripts? Put them in the garbage? You want them back?" I think being dumped by the agent was actually beneficial because it was like, no one gives a crap; no one cares. I had to keep doing it, though no one cared except me.

Mosley: What did you do once you had *The Intuitionist* done?
Whitehead: With this one I was like, I'm gonna chill, I'll get a day job, I'll

revise it really slowly. And someone who read my first book said, "Oh, I heard about your agent dumping you, and I know this woman who you might get along with, so when you're done, why don't you send it to her?" I sent it to this new agent and she liked it, and from then on it was a different story.

On Philosophy and Forgetting

Mosley: Do you consider yourself working within a genre?
Whitehead: I wish. I think it would give me more stability. So far, each book is really different.

Mosley: I think so also. I think it's wonderful. America doesn't have any working philosophers. The closest thing to philosophers in America are novelists, and most novelists are not. But I think that in your work you're looking for the meaning behind actions and behind character and behind even closed doors in some ways. You're looking for reasons. There're existentialist qualities to it. I think you're the first voice in a coming chorus—what I think will be a large chorus—and I think what interests me so much in your work is how thoughtful it is and how incisive it is about not only human motivations but the intelligence behind those motivations. I do see you creating a genre. When I see you compared to Ralph Ellison, I'm not unhappy with that comparison—
Whitehead: Me neither.

Mosley: —because he's a great writer and all that, but also, you know what he's trying to do, honestly and almost without ego, which is interesting—because when you try to understand why things are, you have to remove yourself from it. I think you're very good at that.
Whitehead: If you're going to try and talk about the world, you have to step back. I think that half of being a writer is being outside all the time, but then the other half is trying to bring the world back to the people you're talking about, to your reader, bringing back your reportage—

Mosley: —to the people who are listening. People are listening in on your world.
Whitehead: And then the fact of making real characters, real situations. The distance you've created you're erasing, by trying to make it real for you and real for the reader. So I find it's always this doubling effect where I can

stand back and say, "Oh, that's a *really* well-executed chapter *technically*," and then a couple days later, "Oh, I've actually kind of gotten to something about me or about people that I hadn't thought about."

Mosley: I think the writer writes some small percentage of the book, let's say 20 percent or maybe more, maybe less, depending on how many people read it. Like Shakespeare wrote maybe 2 percent of his books, and the rest of it we've made up over the centuries. Sometimes people come up to me and they'll say, "When Easy or Socrates or whoever went here and did this, I see what you were saying. I interpret that as what's being said is—" Then they outline something, and what they outline is really good. And it's really true and you can see that, hey, that really works, but I didn't mean it. Do you have that feeling ever with your work?

Whitehead: All the time. I think that with *The Intuitionist*, which gets very abstract and was purposefully open to interpretation in a lot of different ways. People will say, "Oh, it's a really great satire on work relations." And I'm like, "Yeah, for twenty pages, but that's not what—"

Mosley: But once you started it, they made the connections from then on. I had written four Easy Rawlins novels before I realized that one of the subjects of my books is black male heroes. I mean, I just never thought of it before. I never thought of it; I never tried to put it down; I never considered it. But one day, I realized, Oh, I'm writing about black male heroes. And then it helped me reinterpret the previous work, and it also sent me in a direction on future work. Even outnumbered, stick to your guns. . . . The first book I wrote was *Gone Fishin'*. I sent it around and, pretty much, people weren't interested in it. They said, "It's good writing; please send us something else—but people are not gonna read this," because they didn't see who the reader was going to be. They said, "You know, white people don't read about black people. Black women don't read about black men and black men don't read, so what are we going to do with your book?" They're wrong—and part of the proof that they're wrong was that the book was written—but that's a whole other thing. And so then I went on and wrote *Devil in a Blue Dress*, and some years later, I published *Gone Fishin'* [1997]. But the thing was, I had an idea when I started writing it: I wanted to talk about the migration of black people from the western South into California, like anybody else talking about their people, their family. One of the ways I see fiction is, you're telling stories of your people and your life.

Whitehead: As I look back over *John Henry Days* and *The Intuitionist* and my first unpublished manuscript, I see a lot more of my upbringing and my experiences begin to take over these weird abstract concepts I start off with. My first manuscript I sent around was a black Gen-X tale that incorporated a lot of pop culture, and a lot of publishers didn't know what to do with it—because it was black twentysomethings hanging out in New York City, and apart from B-boy and romance novels, no one is writing this kind of fun, pop-culture material. When I finished that, I thought, People aren't going to get what I'm writing, so why not just do a crazy elevator inspector book, which is what I want to do, and forget about the whole, "Will publishers like it or not like it?" You just have to do what you have to do. It worked out okay.

Mosley: It worked out fine.

Colson Whitehead

Suzan Sherman / 2001

This interview, "Colson Whitehead" by Suzan Sherman, was commissioned by and first published in *BOMB* magazine 76, Summer 2001. © Bomb Magazine, New Art Publications, and its Contributors. All rights reserved. The BOMB Digital Archive can be viewed at www.bombmagazine.org.

The Intuitionist, Colson Whitehead's acclaimed first novel rests on a completely original premise—elevator inspectors split into two opposing camps. There are the Empiricists (the good-old-boy network of textbook followers) and the Intuitionists (who "intuit" elevator malfunctions and are chided by the Empiricists as "voodoo men" and "witch doctors"). When a new elevator named for Fanny Briggs—a slave who taught herself to read—crashes, Intuitionist Lila Mae, the "first female colored elevator inspector" is scapegoated by the Empiricists for the free fall, and goes undercover to unravel what actually occurred. With consistently elegant prose Whitehead transforms the elevator into a multilayered metaphor for metropolis, religion, race, and upward mobility. Painted in cool shades of gray where urban grit, philosophy, and poetry quietly coexist, *The Intuitionist* is a stunning, mysterious world.

Whitehead continues to explore themes raised in *The Intuitionist* in his much-anticipated new novel, *John Henry Days*, with the folk hero and former slave John Henry, who in the famous race of man versus machine, beats the steam drill and dies afterward. Henry converges with the present day at a John Henry festival, and with J., a black New York journalist who smugly covers the event. In this ambitious novel Whitehead presents a chorus of voices linked to John Henry, weaving the past and present together with confidence. Like the elevator in *The Intuitionist*, the John Henry myth is heightened to take on varied meanings and interpretations, as the recurring replacement of man with machine is explored. Whether it's the dishwasher, Victrola, or the Internet, whether industrial or technological, whether John

Henry or J., the question of "progress" and its startling effects on humanity is raised. Though *John Henry Days* is written in the third person it contains the flavor of oral history, pointing to forgotten moments, gaps in American history, through Whitehead's extraordinary fiction.

Suzan Sherman: There is a grandness, in both scale and subject matter, to *John Henry Days*. No stone is left unturned in tracing a huge chorus of characters who converge on the John Henry legacy. I am reminded of Robert Altman's film *Short Cuts*; the splicing together of lives, a fantastically complex mosaic, though your characters cross centuries. I wonder how you began writing it. Was it with the John Henry myth or with J. the journalist or was it more a conceptual idea?

Colson Whitehead: The book started off conceptually; I wasn't sure how to write about John Henry, though I knew I didn't want to do a historical novel. The early idea was very formal—five-page chapters dealing with different aspects: the history of the steam drill, the Altamont Speedway, and some modern trajectories such as the John Henry stamp ceremony. I plotted it out, but it felt like I hadn't discovered anything new; it seemed too conceptual. I had the great myth of John Henry to jump off of, but no characters, no story. So the real-live historical event of the stamp ceremony became the backbone of the story. J. and his group of hack journalists erupted from there, solidifying the industrial age/information age angle. I fleshed out the town and what would happen over the weekend of the stamp ceremony, and when I did, it became a pretty linear, contemporary story. By forcing these hacks to cover this relatively insignificant event, I found an entry. They were my modern equivalents of the railroad laborers, pick and shovel men of the information age. I wanted to break free of my previous novel, *The Intuitionist*, which is very hermetic; it takes place in one city and has a very small cast. In *John Henry Days* a lot of characters present themselves. As I started to think about the transmission of the John Henry myth and the theme of changing technology, I created characters who would provide footholds for discussing the oral ballad transmission, and then sheet music, the advent of vinyl, and then the late twentieth century where we have all different technological formats for expression.

SS: Initially, why didn't you want to write a historical novel?

CW: It just didn't appeal to me. I wanted to do something where I could talk about modern pop culture. *The Intuitionist* had no pop culture references at all. From being a TV critic and a cultural critic, it felt like an obsession for me. With *John Henry Days* I got my history jones out by having chapters that take place in different time periods.

SS: There is such loving reverence in *The Intuitionist* for the elevator as a grand machine, and the swelling metropolis of skyscrapers it brings. Industry takes on a biological, almost human quality—"a tunnel like a throat," "a stone cocoon," "the skyline rows of broken teeth"—whereas in *John Henry Days* there is an overall disdain for the ever-advancing technology. From the steam drills to Web startups, it's like some sort of amorphous disease. In moving from *The Intuitionist* to writing *John Henry Days*, did you see a thread of continued interest in man's relationship to machine but from an opposing perspective?

CW: I wasn't trying to make a counterpoint to *The Intuitionist*. I definitely have a fascination with machines, the sheer mechanism of the steam drill, the kind of obscure, random invention of the elevator. I like those weird, fun facts. It's only afterwards, now that the book is done and I've read it a couple times . . .

SS: A couple of times? [*laughs*]

CW: Well, yeah. You get a copy of the manuscript and then the galley, each a few months apart, so each reading is like a new experience. You start to love and hate different chapters, and you gain and lose favorite parts. In both cases there's an anxiety about progress and the advancement of machines. Everyone in *The Intuitionist* has all sorts of hopes and aspirations tied into the perfect elevator. In *John Henry Days* it's a lot more diffuse, where you have a songwriter threatened by the mechanization of sheet music, and a blues singer, who makes his living doing concert work, threatened by the advent of the Victrola. There's this anxiety and uneasiness, which I guess is a part of me since it's in both of my books. But technically and structurally, I know exactly why those sections are there.

SS: You mentioned there are parts of *John Henry Days* that you love and parts that you hate. I'm wondering, what are they?

CW: Oh, it varies from week to week. Without getting specific, there are chapters that I can feel proud of because there's a new kind of sentence. It's like, Wow, that's a weird comma-clause-comma construction I haven't done before. Some chapters are just funny, light and lively, and it's a different kind of humor than the rest of the book and what I've done before. There's so many different voices in the book; the stream of consciousness voices were fun to do and worked well, but the following week I thought, Nah, that's kind of mannered. Then next week I change my mind again and think it's great. So I still have a relationship with the book even though it's in the can.

SS: A tremendous amount of research went into *John Henry Days*. Historical references abound, from the steam drill to the Harlem Renaissance to the free Rolling Stones concert at Altamont. Was it a challenge to incorporate history into a fictional narrative without weighing it down; was it some sort of balancing act?
CW: It was definitely a balancing act. Since I didn't write it start-to-finish, I wrote different sections at different times, if I got bored I could take a break doing research for a month before writing another chapter. I'd get five stamp books out of the library and just have a stamp week or a Tin Pan Alley week. Even though I'm kind of a lazy person, I went down to the town of Talcott, West Virginia, where the actual John Henry Days festival takes place every year. I flew to Georgia and my friend picked me up and we drove around in his car for a day and a half. We got a small hotel room in Talcott and walked around, saw the Big Bend Tunnel named in the John Henry ballads. It wasn't something I normally do because I work out of my head. *The Intuitionist* is a book with a lot of small rooms, and *John Henry Days* is a lot bigger; I guess I had to break the mold.

SS: *John Henry Days* begins with people recounting their versions of who they think John Henry is. Each person has a different take on the man, in some cases their point of view is completely tied up with the color of their skin. By beginning the book in such a way, it clearly shows the subjective nature of history, the fluidity of truth, depending upon who tells the story. The idea of truth is also toyed with in *The Intuitionist*, when we learn that Fulton has been keeping the color of his skin a secret. Can you trace when your concern for that sort of truth emerged?
CW: I don't find history very reliable; there's a white history, and there's a black history. And I grew up at a time in college and right after college when there was this crazy deconstructionist sort of thing that nothing exists, everything is fluid, meaning in itself is fluid. It's hard to keep up with everyone's version of the truth; they cancel each other out.

SS: In *John Henry Days* slavery is referenced with a focus on emancipation; that's certainly not the whole truth of what happened in this country.
CW: The end of slavery is not a happy ending; it is not the complete triumph as it's presented in children's schoolbooks. In *The Intuitionist* I left

a lot of things open, like the meaning of the perfect elevator. At different points in the book it means a literal transformation of the city, and then in other parts it's more of a personal transcendence. Then in *John Henry Days* there's the question of whether John Henry existed or not. In the book I talk about the two folklorists who went down to Talcott in the twenties; one guy came away talking to forty people with the idea that he did exist, and two years later, another guy went down and talked to the same people and thought he didn't. The John Henry myth is so ambiguous. He challenges the mechanical steam drill that will replace him to a race; he drills faster and farther and wins, and then he dies from the exertion. So is that a triumph? Is it a defeat? Is it a triumph for the individual, a triumph for the machine, a necessary sacrifice that the community needs? I was trying to emphasize that kind of ambiguity.

SS: Earlier, you said you consider yourself a lazy person. You don't seem that way at all, but, of course, I don't know what you do on a daily basis.

CW: Yeah, you don't want to know. [*laughs*] I write very intensely for, say, six months at a time. And then when I'm not writing, in between books, I take a lot of time off. I'm gestating, thinking about stuff. But I really do plumb the depths of complete slug labor, play a lot of computer solitaire, and catch up on TV. The greatest compliment someone ever gave to me was, "You're the most productive lazy person I know!"

SS: In both books you delve into the self-consciousness of talking about color; not only in terms of white people, but black people as well. Here's a quote: "The biracial who adopted a superficial militancy to overcompensate for light skin discussed the perfidy of ice people with gangster rapper ashamed of a placid upbringing in a middle-class suburb." Your books challenge white presumptions about blackness; I'm thinking about the marketing of your book in the predominantly white publishing industry. What have been your concerns in this regard?

CW: It's being marketed as a literary novel, which is what it is and what I want. Personally, I don't have any gripes the way things are going, though I definitely have gripes with the amount of black fiction being published. In my generation there's me, Paul Beatty, Danzy Senna, and others, and we all do different things. And there are so few black editors around that certain voices aren't getting out there. Then on the other hand, I think there are five new black publishers opening up this year, putting out their particular flavors, so there are ways around the traditional outlets of the commercial publishers.

SS: Were you working on *The Intuitionist* when you were at the *Village Voice*?

CW: I had a TV column there, which gave me a lot of free time. At that point my living expenses were low and I had a really cheap-ass apartment, so I only had to work four days a month. I had time to do my fiction. I did the column for two years, and then I ran out of things to say. I had become a hatchet man, criticizing shows that no one watched anyway, the unseen Fox "Married . . . with Children" spin-off. So I quit that and started *The Intuitionist*. I was freelancing. I was definitely very broke, but I had a lot of time to work on the book.

SS: What did you study at Harvard? Were you a philosophy major?

CW: No, I was an English lit major. There weren't a lot of twentieth-century fiction classes, just the classics. So I spent a lot of time going to the library to look up Ishmael Reed and Thomas Pynchon. Harvard has a really cool drama program with the American Repertory Theatre, so I took a lot of postmodern drama classes. I got this absurdist theater training, which, you know, comes out periodically in different things.

SS: The postal workers.

CW: Yeah, their humor, that Abbott and Costello back and forth.

SS: Your writing makes achingly clear the complexities of black upward mobility. Lila Mae views the first elevator inspector as an Uncle Tom figure, while he feels she's made it because of him. In *John Henry Days*, in the Harlem Renaissance scene, the mother is disgusted to discover her daughter's purchase of black folk music. Blackness is reinterpreted generationally; how heavy is this weight of reinterpretation when you yourself are writing about it?

CW: It's not so much a weight.

SS: Is it a freedom then, to be writing it yourself?

CW: Coming out of the post–Black Arts movement and having blackness being reaffirmed in literature and drama, I think the young black writers of my generation have the freedom to do what we want. I can write a book that uses elevators to talk about race. Or, I can talk about John Henry as a slave doing the only kind of work he can in 1873, and then talk about a privileged middle-class black man in 1996 who chooses his own numbing drudgery. I chose different moments in history to accentuate how issues of race and class have been dealt with; one example being the Strivers Row chapter in *John Henry Days*, where the bourgeois mom forbids any street Negroness in the house, to the point of erasing the black contribution to pop music.

SS: There is no written account from that time of John Henry having beaten the steam drill—there is only oral history. For many reasons it's been imperative for blacks to assert what's been left out of history books. Were you thinking along those lines in terms of the Intuitionists, those who intuit what something is; they feel it, without relying on textbook facts?
CW: Maybe, unconsciously.

SS: Your narratives have a wonderful zigzagging quality. The plot is in a progression, but it's not anything that's expected. There's a scene in *John Henry Days* where a girl gets an internship at a newspaper, which she ends up resenting because all her friends go to Europe that summer. This girl does not show up again in the rest of the novel; I kept expecting her to reemerge. What was the decision in bringing her up and letting her go?
CW: In terms of the story itself, there are chapters that serve to further the story of what happened during the John Henry Days stamp festival weekend, and then there are chapters which serve to further the advancement of different notions of John Henry, what John Henry–ness is to different people.

SS: And the notion of what journalism is becoming, its elitism.
CW: Yeah, she's a part of the journalistic hackery world; the dilettante intern. She doesn't come back because I feel like she served her purpose. A lot of the characters show up and don't come back or come back only in references or come back as ghosts in other characters' stories.

SS: You chose to center the book on a postage stamp festival honoring the John Henry stamp. Despite all the technological advances, there are still some things, like postage stamps, which are steeped in nostalgia. When you were writing were you thinking at all about this, as a contrast to the ever-advancing technology?
CW: I think for me, the nostalgia comes out in different ways; the town of Talcott embraces the one-hundred-twenty-year-old myth as a cause for celebration. The John Henry Days Festival actually exists.

SS: Is that when you went down there?
CW: No, I went down in the off-season. [*laughs*] I'm pretty sure the festival in my book is a lot bigger and definitely more lethal than theirs. In the face

of rapid growth of these mono cities, these edge cities, where every town has a Gap, and we're all connected through the media. We're united in a mass-produced culture, and then there's this nostalgia for things we never had. You get that tension in Lucien, the PR guru who goes down to Talcott, he's not really sure what to make of all this authentic sentiment. He wants to embrace it, but can only think in a corrupt way. He doesn't know what to make of these strange feelings of community and loss. Because I grew up in Manhattan, I have a lot of weird notions about small-town life. It was definitely fun for me to go to Talcott and try to create a few characters in opposition to the cynical, urban Lucien.

SS: There's the husband and wife who run the motel that everyone stays in. Did these characters emerge as you were going along?

CW: Yeah. I had a semi-outline. The more research I did, the more I wanted to expand on the myth. I put in Guy Johnson, the black folklorist who goes down there in the twenties, I put in Paul Robeson because he's such an incredible figure, and then I found out he was in a John Henry play on Broadway. I definitely had to reign myself in because it just became a kitchen sink, anything that mentioned John Henry I wanted to put in. [*laughs*] The one thing I'm sorry I didn't put in was a Johnny Cash chapter because he has this John Henry song which is pretty cool. He sang it one day on a variety show in the seventies and misidentified the town as Beckley, West Virginia. The residents of Talcott were very upset, and so he paid for the John Henry monument in Talcott. It would be incredibly cool to write about Johnny Cash, but it seemed like I had enough as it was.

SS: Was it easier writing the second book with all the acclaim you received for *The Intuitionist*, or did that make the writing, the living up to something, all the more difficult?

CW: I was lucky that I wrote half the book before *The Intuitionist* came out.

SS: Lazy you!

CW: Lazy me. [*laughs*] So what happened was I wrote half of *John Henry Days*, we moved back to New York, *The Intuitionist* came out, and I didn't actually work on the book for a year. I knew exactly what was going to happen in it; I had the voices down, though that wasn't what was weighing on my mind, anxiety-wise. *John Henry Days* is such a different book, stylistically and structurally, from *The Intuitionist*. I just hadn't done anything like it before; that was more my worry rather than can I live up to the good reviews of *The Intuitionist*.

SS: In *John Henry Days* you describe the writer Bob the newcomer, his debut, then Bob's return as "the second novel, recapitulating some of the first's themes, somehow lacking—emboldened by success tries to tackle too much." Do you have different fears on the publication of your second book?

CW: I'm fearless. [*laughs*] I attracted a lot of mystery fans with *The Intuitionist* because of its structure, so I'm not sure if they're going to be coming along for the ride this time. But I think it will attract different people for being a very different book.

SS: Do you have an ideal audience?

CW: I have a few friends who read all my stuff, works in progress. I think about what they might say, their predilections, but my ideal reader is me. [*laughs*] I guess the effort's wasted, since I'm actually writing it. But someone like me, or younger, who hasn't been exposed to crazy, more contemporary fiction, or who might want to start writing. For me, it's been important when I've encountered particular books in my life like *Invisible Man* at the age of twenty, or *Gravity's Rainbow*, as I started to write and to learn what I could and couldn't do.

SS: Do you remember what you were told you couldn't do?

CW: In sophomore English, reading Jane Austen all the time, you think that's what literature is. I don't worry about following some sort of Dickensian structure I learned in high school. The canon is not all that it's cracked up to be—there's a lot more out there.

SS: Do you like Ben Katchor's cartoons?

CW: Oh yeah, I've always felt a real affinity. His New York is the New York I love, the sort of fictional New York I never lived in, the buildings below 30th Street that I got from growing up with *The Twilight Zone*, and the beleaguered guys in fedoras who are shoe salesmen and ventriloquists—all the weird, kind of Broadway, shticky 42nd Street, sad characters living in this sort of pug-nosed world. I'm not really sure why I latched onto that as an interesting place or landscape, but Ben Katchor really captures it.

SS: I'm going to a lecture of his tomorrow night on museum cafeterias of the world. [*laughs*] In *The Intuitionist* Lila Mae is described as the first female colored elevator inspector. Do you see yourself as a "first" in some way?

CW: The first colored novelist to write about elevators.

SS: Maybe on a more personal level?

CW: Well, I think I'm trying to do what's not expected.

SS: What do you think is expected?

CW: When I started writing, the twenty-something, angsty-struggle, first novel would come into the *Voice* all the time. It was the slacker moment. And that was what I didn't want to do; I wanted to make it new. It's the way my mind works; I can't write any other way. I don't worry about staking a claim for myself because what I end up writing is freaky in conception and readable in execution, at least I hope so.

SS: Numerous male authors are accused of focusing predominantly on male characters and concerns in their books, but you've painted consistently strong, independent female characters. In an interview you gave for *Salon* you mentioned that Lila Mae had initially been a man. Did you choose to make her a woman to further separate her from the good-old-boy world of the Empiricists?

CW: Once the character became female that came into play, but it was more just trying to not do what was comfortable. When I first finished the manuscript for *The Intuitionist* the main character was a wise-talking, young guy. And after reading a page of it, I was like, who cares? So I said, female character. Let's stretch it, not make it first person. Both those things, a third person book and a female character just seemed more interesting; it made the book more fun to do than something I already know. In the same way that *John Henry Days* started as gemlike essays on facets of John Henry. Once you think it up, why do something you already know you can do?

SS: I imagine it would not be as fun for the reader either.

CW: Yeah, that's more of a secondary concern. It's just less fun to write. If there's no challenge, there's no point in doing it.

SS: Does being a writer make sense to you in relation to your familial history? Were you one of those people who planned on becoming a writer when they were six years old?

CW: I was in the seventh or eighth grade. I thought it would be cool to write big geeky, slasher, horror, sci-fi movies—*Blade Runner, The Shining*—or be a comic book writer. I was living in a kind of fantasy world. My parents wanted me to do something more stable, lawyering or doctoring, but they got off my back when I started working for the *Voice*. As a kid in New York I always wanted to write for the *Voice*. Every week I went to the back pages to see which band was playing, then went to Irving Plaza and the Ritz, and read the music reviews afterwards. I became a sort of *Voice* addict.

SS: Intuitionism, the ability to feel without having to see is described by the Empiricists as "downright voodoo." I'm curious about your own religious upbringing.
CW: Did we practice voodoo? I guess my mom went to church as a child and started going again a few years ago. We were not a religious household when I was growing up. We were agnostics or atheists; I'm not sure which.

SS: Skeptics.
CW: We were a very skeptical household.

SS: Why in *The Intuitionist* did you choose to make the metropolis "the most famous city in the world," as opposed to simply Manhattan, and why not place it in a specific time? Did the choice of leaving it vague, sort of Kafkaesque, have to do with giving the story more reverberation in relationship to today?
CW: I wanted it to start as a parody of a detective story. I wanted this noirish city to work in, and then as different themes began to develop I started playing around with Lila Mae as a civil rights baby thrust into a completely male workplace. It became advantageous and fun to have a timeless locale where creatively I wasn't pinned down. Also the story is so fantastic, like a parallel world of New York that exists only on certain street corners at certain times of day. As the story became more allegorical, it seemed like the right choice.

SS: Did it feel like a relief then, when *John Henry* became incredibly specific?
CW: Oh, totally, yeah. There was one thing I couldn't figure out how to shoehorn in: Flight 800, the New York-to-Paris plane that went down in August of 1996. I thought it would be interesting to have one of the junketeers on that plane, since they're such doomed mercenaries. It fit in with the undercurrent of modern violence in *John Henry Days*. It was great to put real life names in the book instead; to be able to say he walked down Broadway as opposed to the great boulevard. And then being able to bring in Paul Robeson or the Eleanor Bumpurs case or Altamont—real-life scenes that glance off the themes in *John Henry Days*. It was totally fun, and liberating.

SS: Here's a question about endings. *The Intuitionist* concludes with Lila Mae sitting down to write her own words, and *John Henry Days* ends with

J. almost certainly going off with the woman he's grown fond of—the "real story," as he calls it—as opposed to remaining on his sorry press junket. Do you consciously see your novels as ending on hopeful notes, and are you yourself hopeful in regard to the future?

CW: It's funny because in both books, different people interpret the endings in different ways. It seems that the more pessimistic you are, the more optimistic you find the endings of both books, and the more optimistic you are, the more pessimistic you find the endings.

SS: Hmm. [*laughs*]

CW: I thought of both J. and Lila Mae as writers: Lila Mae writing *The Last Elevator* and having a room of her own, being apart from the world in order to create, and J. having his existential dilemma about writing and if it's worthwhile. For me, personally, I summon those feelings for the books apart from their constructions. I find both endings to be both optimistic and open-ended, but then people read them and seem really upset.

SS: What could possibly be upsetting about them?

CW: Well, people say Lila Mae's all alone, everybody hates her, she has no friends, and she's stuck in this small room overlooking a factory. Nobody understands what she's doing for many years—which is actually a writer's dilemma; you're writing something, and it might get published, it might not. And if it does no one buys it and you struggle, and maybe one day someone will actually dig it. With *John Henry Days*, without trying to spell out the ending, it's a question of whether J. is fated in the same way John Henry is, to meet a certain course of action, or can J. escape the loop that seems to be his destiny? I got calls from some people who said, "I finished the book and the ending is so sad. God, I'm so depressed." And other people said the complete opposite.

SS: Do you like the variety of interpretation?

CW: Yes, I feel pretty hands-off once it's done.

SS: But was that your intention?

CW: Yes, it was more intentional with *John Henry Days*. It's what I wanted.

SS: In the face of all the acclaim you received with *The Intuitionist* and that you will certainly receive for *John Henry Days*, you have such a humility about you. How have you maintained this sense of yourself?

CW: Well, my attitude is that, hopefully, I'll be writing books for a while, and they won't all be as well received as *The Intuitionist*. You have ups and downs. They'll all be received differently, I'll have different experiences writing them, and they'll serve different purposes for me creatively. I'm glad people can read them and have different responses.

SS: Do you have another book in the works—being that you're so lazy?

CW: I've started a book which you could say is about the Band-Aid industry. It's pretty fun, and I'll leave it at that.

Writing Home

Evette Porter / 2002

From *Black Issues Book Review* 4.2 (May–June 2002): 36–37. Reprinted with permission of Blanche Evette Porter.

Every writer has a place they call home. For James Baldwin, it was Harlem. For Zora Neale Hurston, it was Eatonville, Florida. Whether consciously or intuitively, that sense of place invariably creeps into an author's writing. Walter Mosley's Easy Rawlins novels are set in Los Angeles—the city where he grew up—replete with familiar landmarks and references that native Angelenos easily recognize. For Colson Whitehead, author of *John Henry Days* and his first novel, *The Intuitionist*, home is New York City.

Born in Manhattan, the thirty-two-year-old Whitehead has lived all over the city. "We were a family of renters," he says of his childhood. "Every three years, depending on fortune and how many kids were in the house, we'd move up and down Manhattan. I was born on 139th [Street] and Riverside, and we lived there until I was in kindergarten," he recalls. "Then we moved a couple of times, until finally in high school, I ended up on 101st and West End Avenue. All of these different neighborhoods—the East Side, the Upper West Side, Harlem—they've left their mark on me."

For the past eight years though, Whitehead has lived in Fort Greene, Brooklyn, a neighborhood that has recently undergone the kind of demographic changes that gentrification engenders. Although the house he lives in with his wife, Natasha, has the hardscrabble look of a clapboard row house in need of a little paint, it possesses the kind of charm that reflects the optimism of the neighborhood, easily fitting in with the trendy restaurants a couple of blocks away and the bodegas around the corner.

"I'm definitely a New Yorker," says Whitehead. "I've tried living other places, but I always end up coming back here. It's always nice to walk around the neighborhood and say, 'Oh yeah, that's the cramped apartment where I wrote *The Intuitionist*. Or, that's 757 Fulton where I wrote half of *John Henry*

Days,'" he says. "All of these places have an additional layer of meaning for me because where I write is so tied to the book—the memory of writing in certain rooms, on certain tables."

In *The Intuitionist*, a novel about a black elevator inspector Lila Mae Watson, the story takes place amid the kind of urban architecture—skyscrapers and congested spaces—much like Manhattan. "I was broke and living in a really small place," says Whitehead, describing the period when he was writing the novel. "I think that's why Lila Mae Watson, in *The Intuitionist*, ends up in a series of very tiny rooms," he says.

"I always try and put some Brooklyn names in my book," he adds. "The big elevator inspector, who is a theorist and an Intuitionist, is named Fulton, and that's because I wrote the book on Fulton Street. Every time I'd look out the window, it would enter the book."

In *John Henry Days*, Whitehead takes the story of the familiar black folk hero John Henry, who prevails in a contest against a steam drill and afterward dies of exhaustion, and turns it into a metaphor about the machine age versus the information age. In the novel, a young black freelance journalist from New York named J. Sutter heads to West Virginia on a junket to cover a backwater media event called "John Henry Days," a festival celebrating a new postage stamp in honor of the famous steel-driver.

"There's an encounter that J. Sutter has with this crackhead that was drawn from my own experience with a pretty well-known crackhead in the neighborhood," says Whitehead. In real life, he says, the guy was arrested and offered the choice of going to jail or entering rehab. "He entered rehab, and now he has a job reconditioning these brownstones that people are buying. He has his own construction business, owns a house, and has put on, like, two hundred pounds. It's somewhat parallel with the ongoing gentrification of the neighborhood," he observes.

"I saw him one day, and I didn't recognize him," he says of the real-life former drug abuser. "He came up to me and said, 'Hey, I remember you. Remember me?' It was kind of an awkward exchange," says Whitehead. "He said, 'I just want to apologize.'"

Right now Whitehead is working on a book of essays about New York, due out next spring. "I started them when I finished *John Henry Days*, and I was still in writing mode," he says.

"I just started writing, not knowing what these pieces were about. I did a piece about Central Park, and I did one about the Port Authority," he says. "For research, I walk around and just take notes and try to eavesdrop on the city. So I've been walking around and trying to get a feel for how people experience these New York places like Central Park or the Brooklyn Bridge."

As for the allure of his hometown Whitehead says, "I think I identify myself with the metropolis. But America is bigger than the seven-mile strip of Manhattan. So partially, I'm trying to figure out how I fit into America through these different people."

Educating the Imagination: Colson Whitehead

Matthew Sharpe / 2003

Reprinted from *Teachers & Writers Magazine* (Vol. 30, No. 3, 2003) by permission of Teachers & Writers Collaborative.

Matthew Sharpe: In *John Henry Days* you use a variety of forms of speech: a montage of letters, a post office publicity pamphlet, a stamp collector's newsletter, a magazine puff piece, a newspaper article about a shooting at a public event, "John Henry" song lyrics, passages written in the form of a play. Can you talk about this approach to writing a novel?

Colson Whitehead: My first book, *The Intuitionist*, is very hermetic: mostly you're following Lila Mae in the deep dark city, and there's a pretty consistent tone. In *John Henry Days* I wanted to have a lot more voices. Each new character or situation would dictate the way I'd have to tell it. So when, say, the two post office workers are chatting in a bar, I didn't want to write, "He put his arm down on the bar and picked up a beer." I wanted to get this kind of Abbott-and-Costello back-and-forth. It seemed the best way to do that was as a play. It reminds me of being a journalist. Writing for the *Village Voice* and different magazines, you have to figure out what the style is for each editor and each section of each magazine. Each situation and character demands a certain kind of voice, and special care.

MS: Sometimes I feel the characters being shoved aside by all the different discourses. You've got this character Lucien, an über-publicist, who says, "Air is an admixture of nitrogen, oxygen, trace gases, and one of these trace gases is American cliché and we breathe it in with our first breath." So I felt the various jargons of the book constituted one of the metaphorical machines that the protagonist J. Sutter, a pop journalist, is fighting against. Does anybody ever win against that machine?

CW: I think J. Sutter starts off as a pretty disreputable character, and part of what I was trying to do in the middle of the book is to make the reader care about him more and become invested in whether he can pull out of the cycle of press junkets he's in. So I think the point of the ending is that I leave it up to you, the reader, to decide. And I have one response as the writer who has piled grief upon misfortune upon horrible event on these characters for three hundred pages. But then as a reader and an optimistic person, I have my own interpretation that's separate from that of the person who's written the book. When I put that hat on, I feel hopeful about J. But I have these contradictory impulses, the readerly one and the writerly one; how you feel about characters versus what you have the characters do.

MS: What's the difference?
CW: You want characters to live and breathe, but you are actually making them do things. They don't have free will. They are serving a function, to put it very baldly.

MS: Why is it good to end the novel without our knowing for sure what happens to the protagonist?
CW: That kind of ambiguity is at the heart of the John Henry myth. When I was first thinking of it as something to write about, my interpretation was that it was a triumph for humanity: he beats the steam drill and he dies, but, you know, "Good job."

In the first references to John Henry I came across, he'd been claimed by socialists as a working-class hero who strikes a blow against the capitalist machine. But as I began doing more research, I found that for some steel workers it was a cautionary tale. He was too proud: "This hammer killed John Henry but, it won't kill me," they sing. In some versions the fight with the machine is a very small part and—he's more of a swaggering playboy who has a lot of ladies—and his last adventure is with a machine and he dies, but that's part of a portrait of a larger-than-life rascal.

So if I'd ended the book one way, it would have been me, the author, putting my stamp on something that's too mutable and uncontrollable, and would not have been in keeping with the story. Plus, it's fun to make people work.

MS: Your first novel, *The Intuitionist*, is a detective novel of sorts. Did you know who'd done it before you started writing?
CW: I knew a lot of it. There's a twist or two in the middle that I hadn't thought out. There are many betrayals in the book, and I'm sure some of

them weren't there at the beginning. I did study the structure of a lot of detective movies and the neodetective novels of Ellroy and Leonard and Mosley, and when you read these books back to back, the structures become more obvious. You know that in an Elmore Leonard novel, twenty pages form the end, bad guy number two will get killed. So when I was plotting my book, I had a certain number of conventional detective flourishes or beats, and then a few crept in later when I thought I didn't have enough or I wanted to make it even more confusing for people.

MS: *The Intuitionist* features elevated trains and rotary phones. You even refer to "gathering integration." On the wall of one character's office there's a picture of someone you describe as "the famous reverend, the man who was so loud down South," and African Americans are called "coloreds." Did you have a particular year in mind?

CW: No year. The twentieth century. Mixing and matching these different chronological bits forces the reader to wonder what year we are in. If Lila Mae—who I see as a contemporary of mine, a civil rights person—is in this pre–civil rights workplace where the old boys' network is in place, what does that mean? Black people are colored: what does that mean when we also have these supertechnological elevators in which people are rushing around? I think there's an interesting tension when you can't pin it down, and there are these different kinds of inputs that are telling you one thing on one page and another thing on another page. I think that that confusion mimics racial confusion at large in the country. Has civil rights happened, or has it not happened? You can read the newspaper and feel that same confusion.

MS: Passing seems to be a big literal and metaphorical phenomenon in *The Intuitionist*.

CW: In black literature of the late nineteenth and early twentieth centuries, passing was such a cliché plot device that it seemed fun to put it in there. And in detective stories, everyone's always passing: passing for good, presenting themselves as good and decent when they're not. The damsel in distress, the politician, the real estate developer. So it seemed like a detective novel trope. Then as I developed the two schools of elevator inspection, Empiricism and Intuitionism—seeing things on the surface as opposed to what's beneath—it seemed to work more. It's always accidental, I think. You start with a very simple idea, and the more you think about it, the more changes you can ring on it. And the accidental choice you make—like, say, elevators—can turn out to be a rich metaphor: something that elevates, uplifts the race.

MS: Here's an interesting quote from *The Intuitionist* about Fulton, who wrote the first book about Intuitionist elevator inspection. "Fulton's words discovered and altered Lila Mae in her early studies." Have you ever had an experience like that?

CW: Reading *Invisible Man* in college. In terms of highbrow black literature, I'd only read certain novels of protest that were very realistic. And then I read *Invisible Man*, which was totally out there and bugged out. It opens with the protagonist in a room with a thousand light bulbs. He works in a white paint factory. He lives underground. There's a satchel with a letter inside that says, "Keep this nigger running." The book is so strange. I remember thinking, "You can do that? In books?" I felt the same way when I was reading *Gravity's Rainbow*. When I was coming to the end I thought, He's not going to wrap this up, is he? HE'S NOT GOING TO WRAP THIS UP, IS HE? I can't believe he did that! It was a revelation that you can be unconventional in subject—say, in *Invisible Man*—and you can be unconventional in structure—say, in *Gravity's Rainbow*—and have it all work and be a great piece of art. I was a sophomore in college when I read both of those. Good year for me.

MS: Lila Mae of *The Intuitionist* is so different from J. Sutter of *John Henry Days*. What made you switch from one to the other?

CW: Maybe this can become a question about pedagogy. From book to book I want to do something different. If I know it's going to be hard, that makes me want to do it.

Before I wrote *The Intuitionist*, I wrote a more stereotypical book, pop culture—heavy, taking place in New York in the present. And the cast was very much like me. And when I started *The Intuitionist* I wanted to do something very different. So: third-person narrator, female character—I haven't done those two before, can I do them? And when I started *John Henry Days*, I already knew I could do a linear, plot-heavy book, so how about a book with a more thematic plot that has a lot more characters than just this one repressed, controlled character and a lot of different voices. I know I can do Lila Mae, and I know I can do a New York hipster. But can I do a railroad baron or a PR guru or a young girl in the forties on Striver's Row? I think the fear keeps you honest. Not knowing if you can do it makes the work better because you're always second-guessing yourself, making sure you're doing the best work that you can—not coasting.

I just started teaching fiction this year, and someone gave me three stories. And they're all in the same tone, and they're all kind of perfect. But if you know you can do it, why write the fourth story in that style? You have this voice down, so stop doing it. That's the advice I give to people: this is a really good story, don't do it again. Figure out what you don't want to do, and do that.

MS: You told me earlier that you were embittered when you were writing *The Intuitionist.* You were so young. What were you embittered about?

CW: Writing a first novel that no one liked. Twenty-six publishers. My agent dumped me. It's daunting to know it's going to take a year and a half, two years, three years before the next book is done, and you've got to get back on the horse. I'm always excited to start a new book, and then I'm like, "This is not going to be done for two years. This is a horrible, horrible, horrible business." Obviously it's very rewarding, and I love doing it. I'm happy when I'm in the work, and I have a good day. But not getting support from an institution—you're not in an MFA program, you write short stories that aren't getting taken by journals, you're broke—you know, typical artist complaints, that's where I was. And it was hard to realize that the only thing that would make it right was to write another one.

MS: You didn't go to an MFA program.

CW: No. I was writing articles for the *Village Voice* for five years, and I worked out a lot of bad habits and had a lot of feedback. When you write a dud article you know it's a dud. And when you write a good one you get a lot of reinforcement. I felt I could apply to grad school, or I could just write the book. I was a freelancer and was enough of a regular at the *Voice* that I didn't have to hustle for work. I had three weeks out of the month to work on my own stuff. So I figured, why go back to school? I hated school. The older I got, the more—well, maybe I can't say this because this is *Teachers & Writers.*

MS: Yes, you can.

CW: I got to the point of, "Just give me the books; send me the exam. I'll fill it out and send it back to you." That's how I felt at the end of my college years. I think I was kind of done with it.

MS: Did you have any good experiences as a student that have helped you as a writer?

CW: When I went to college I tried to get into the creative writing classes, and I was never accepted. I wrote these crappy little stories. I think the lack of support was actually helpful in that you have to really decide you want to do it, and you do it despite any number of setbacks. And then there are setbacks in the publishing world, and then there's writing stories that don't work. This will be ongoing in the writing life. And when you get used to being disappointed, the recovery time gets shorter, the time you need before you get back to work gets shorter and shorter.

Post Office to Unveil Colson Whitehead Stamp

"Dave" / 2006

From the *PowellsBooks.Blog* (October 10, 2006) on the powells.com website. Reprinted with permission.

Talcott, West Virginia, is the site of the first annual John Henry Days festival, celebrating the US Postal Service's new folk heroes stamp series, among whose four figures is none other than John Henry, the nineteenth-century black laborer reputed to have defeated a steam engine in a steel-driving contest here only to die from exhaustion before he could celebrate the victory.

J. Sutter, junketeer extraordinaire, has come to cover the event for a new travel website. Jaded, road-weary, and hyperconscious of his race among hillside Confederate flags, J.'s weekend adventure supplies the primary forward track of Colson Whitehead's second novel, as well as a platform from which to satirize the American media's servitude to capitalist enterprise and the public's eagerness to swallow its pitches whole.

Yet perhaps only half of the novel follows the events of the festival weekend. The balance is built upon short sections wherein Whitehead confronts the John Henry myth directly, via both re-creations of work scenes on the C&O Railroad's Big Bend Tunnel project and brief portraits of lives somehow touched by the legend: a Chicago bluesman for whom the hero's ballad provides a first opportunity to record on vinyl, a crack addict eighty years later deliriously singing the chorus, a reclusive collector of John Henry memorabilia whose museum boasts the largest collection of pieces in the world yet never once attracts a visitor.

"Whitehead's accomplished debut, *The Intuitionist* (1998), earned him a Whiting Writers' Award, and he now presents an even more sagacious tale, an inventive, funny, and bittersweet inquiry into the significance of folk hero John Henry," Donna Seaman of *Booklist* wrote. "Masterfully composed and full of myth and magic, Whitehead's great American novel considers such dualities as nature and civilization, legend and history, black and white, and altruism and greed, while deftly skewering the absurdities of the information age."

The highly anticipated follow-up to Whitehead's revered debut, *John Henry Days* is either a remarkable historical novel, an illuminating counterpoint of Reconstruction Then and Now, or the year's most spot-on contemporary satire, depending where you look.

Dave: Why John Henry?

Colson Whitehead: I always liked him. I first heard about him as a kid, and there weren't a lot of black superheroes growing up. Marvel Comics had their Falcon and Luke Cage, but the story always struck a chord with me.

When I finished *The Intuitionist* I had this vague idea that I'd write about John Henry, but no peg. So I thought, Update for the information age, and I took it from there. I knew I wanted to talk about the myth, and as I did more research I started to compose an outline. Different things would allow me to address different parts of the myth.

Dave: It's a lot more than John Henry's story.

Whitehead: I was trying, over the course of the book, to explore the *idea* of John Henry, to attack it from different angles, different ways people interact with the myth. The blues singer trying to get on vinyl. The sheet music guy working for Tin Pan Alley publishers. And, indirectly, J.'s aunt, Jennifer Sutter, who comes across the sheet music. For her it raises class issues, the new black bourgeoisie in the forties.

John Henry becomes a way to talk about different things and different things become a way to talk about John Henry. It goes back and forth.

Dave: You mentioned elsewhere seeing a cartoon about John Henry as a child. Your teacher showed a film in class.

Whitehead: It was the multicultural seventies, and he was trying to show how different cultures are woven into the American fabric. I was in fourth grade. I wanted to re-create that scene because it was my first John Henry exposure.

Dave: The John Henry legend intrudes on characters' lives in completely different ways. Some of the intrusions become meaningful in the character's life, others don't stick at all.

Whitehead: There's a chapter where J. is writing in Brooklyn, and he meets this crackhead stumbling around his block. The crackhead, in his delirium, is singing the ballad.

A popular song can, as if on the radio, come into the room, hit the back of your consciousness, and float away. J. has no solid tie to John Henry until he goes to West Virginia and begins to remember how it's linked up with his life.

Dave: I'm not sure when I first heard the story. A couple years ago here at Powell's, I came across a children's book about it, but I'm sure I'd heard of it before.

Whitehead: When I talk to people now, it's interesting to hear their reaction. Oh, John Henry . . . was he a president? I make a steel-driving motion with my hands, and they might remember the song. "There's a song about him, right?"

Dave: Who won the race? Did John Henry flat-out win? Or did he not win because the exertion killed him? What's the moral? Did you have any kind of opinion about that as you began writing? Did your perspective change as you wrote?

Whitehead: When I started, I hadn't really thought about it for a while. I thought it was a triumph. But as I did more research, I started to recall the central ambiguity of the story, which I think is why I gravitated toward it. Different characters espouse their point-of-view, whether or not it was a triumph of the individual. For me, I still have no idea what the hell the John Henry story means, even now.

Dave: Do you read what people are writing about your books?

Whitehead: The first few reviews, I'm anxious to see how they're going to fall. After that, it's easier to wait. But the first couple days I'm feverishly going on the web to see what people are saying.

Dave: I stumbled over a couple points John Updike made in the *New Yorker*. In his conclusion, he refers to a line in the novel where you say that J. stands there "as if choices are possible." Updike wrote, "If choices aren't possible, why is [J.] taking up space in the middle of a work of fiction?" What about that?

Whitehead: Choices might be possible. The novel, itself, has two possible endings, and readers fall into one of two camps deciding whether J. can galvanize himself and move on. J. is not really a Hamlet-like character, but *to be or not to be*, people have posed that question before. I'm not inventing a new sort of character. Inertial characters, since World War II, are pretty common. What a character *isn't* doing is as important as taking action.

Also, in the last line of his review, Updike writes that J. Sutter "is no John Henry." That's a line from the book, actually. I don't think he remembered it. I'm opposing this jaded, late-twentieth-century journalist with the superdynamic John Henry. Yes, that's the opposition set up from the very first chapter.

Dave: I do feel like there's a certain divide. I didn't feel like Updike read the story as you were writing it. At one point he complains that "J. need not be black at all."
Whitehead: He didn't really grasp certain things about the book. He says a lot of nice things—I'm not trying to slag him—but there's stuff he didn't get.

Dave: It's clear that each reader is taking a somewhat different story from it. Is it a story about J.? Is it a story about John Henry? Where is the center of this story exactly? Was there any particular item you used as ballast?
Whitehead: No one set thing. Some people gravitate more toward J. as an anchor for the book and others like the John Henry historical parts more. My ideal reader sees how both play and interact.

Dave: Some reviewers have called this book's structure fragmented; one called the digressions vignettes; someone else called them filaments. No one seems to agree what they are, but clearly there's no center into which they can easily settle.
Whitehead: As opposed to *The Intuitionist*, which has a solid plot, structurally a take-off on the detective novel: an elevator crashes; how did it happen? This has a more thematic plot. I'm advancing the story by advancing various points-of-view of John Henry, going back and forth between the story of the weekend and the story of the dissemination of the John Henry legend.

Dave: One thing that really impressed me were the swings in tone. Historical, then contemporary. Dry, then really funny.
Whitehead: There's a lot more comedy in the book than I think one would gather from reading the reviews.

Dave: We've already used one funny clip on the website: J. eyeing the prime rib at the weekend's first buffet dinner. But other scenes, too: Pamela's temp job for an Internet start-up, the New York publicity parties, the whole junketeering conceit, and the idea of "The List." One of the fundamental undertones J. brings to the novel is that he distrusts narrative completely. It's all contrived. Every written document is formulated to produce an effect. I found his worldview hysterical in that respect.

Whitehead: He's a sad character, but he has a funny take on the world. The problem is to reel in the cynical, sarcastic person and try to make him sympathetic as the weekend goes on and his dilemma becomes more apparent. I find it compelling, but I can see how people initially wouldn't like him much.

Part of the problem for me was to figure out how I'd act in these scenarios, a black New Yorker going down South for the first time. There was such a thing as slavery at one time. There are those Confederate flags waving in the wind, so I use his paranoia of lynchings and so forth, exaggerations of how I'd feel down there.

Dave: I took to J. as a character almost immediately—not that I liked him, but I *enjoyed* him. I wanted to read more about him. For me, the John Henry pieces only became more meaningful later, by accumulation.

Whitehead: That's what I was going for. The first chapter is all about J., getting the characters to the town. Then it starts spiraling off. Each bit about John Henry, hopefully, advances your idea of him a little more, bit by bit, until you've taken him out of the heroic role of racing a steam drill and reduced him to human scale. Meanwhile you've elevated other characters to something like heroic status, the blues singer or the Tin Pan Alley guy.

Dave: Characters appear and suddenly withdraw four pages later. As a writer, that means you're allowing yourself four or five pages to create a meaningful, memorable character, starting from scratch over and over again.

Whitehead: It's fun in a way. I don't have a knack for writing short stories. Maybe some chapters could stand alone, but a lot of those vignettes need the others to make them shine. I don't write from start to finish. If I know who a character is, I can write that chapter when I get to it. If I don't, I can wait six months and, hopefully, at that point, I'll know who the person is. There were times when I wasn't ready to tackle a character and I had to wait. That was the hard part. I knew what function they had to serve for the story, but I didn't know their dialogue or what made them tick.

Dave: Lucien is one of my favorite minor characters. There's actually quite a lot of build-up—characters talking and speculating about him—before we meet him. His chapter was hilarious.

Whitehead: Thanks. I've started reading his monologue at events. Writing that monologue was really fun.

Dave: Before *The Intuitionist*, you worked at the *Village Voice* as a television critic. That seems funny to me in the context of your literary success. Appropriate, maybe, but funny.

Whitehead: I loved doing the TV column. The way I ran it, TV became a way to talk about anything. During an election, you could talk about election coverage, then talk about Democrats and Republicans. If Flight 800 goes down, you can talk about media coverage, how catastrophic events create a certain kind of discourse, a viewership over the course of a news cycle.

After two years, I burned out. There weren't enough new shows to keep me enthusiastic, but I don't really see a division between high and low. I think *The Sopranos* is up there with any Hollywood product. I find TV very interesting. I still avidly watch my favorite shows.

Dave: Are you interested in writing for other venues? Stage? Film? Television?

Whitehead: I started writing a play, actually, last month, coming out of the Lucien monologue, and there are some chapters in play form in *John Henry Days*. I like having that back-and-forth play of dialogue.

I was in the middle of another novel when I started doing this publicity stuff, so I figured, "Well, if I can't really work, I'll start writing a play. It'll be fun."

Dave: Is that novel you mention the book about Band-Aids I heard you were working on?

Whitehead: It is, yes. The play is too bizarre to talk about at this point.

Dave: Okay, but the Band-Aid one sounds pretty normal, so maybe we can talk about that. What are you writing about Band-Aids?

Whitehead: It's probably too early to talk about it, but I think it kind of links up with *The Intuitionist*, taking a mundane thing and thinking about it too much. After a while, you have something to work with.

Dave: *The Intuitionist* is a great book to recommend because all you have to tell someone is that it's about warring schools of elevator inspectors. Not many books are so easy to sum up in such an intriguing way. How did you wind up writing that?

Whitehead: I'd written a manuscript that didn't go anywhere. It meandered too much. So I wanted to see if I could write a plot, and a detective story has a lot of real backbone to work with. I thought it would be a parody of a detective novel, having an escalator inspector solve a crime. I'd seen a bit on

TV about escalator inspectors and thought, What a weird job. Being in New York, I turned it into elevators instead.

Doing more research, I began to make up a culture for them. Once you make up a school, there's naturally going to be infighting and opposing philosophies, so I created the Empiricists and the Intuitionists. It evolved by trying to create an elevator world. There would be a father figure who laid down a founding philosophy—well, who's that? How does he fit in? How does Lila Mae fit into the prevailing wisdom as a rebel? It really just evolved from trying to write a fake detective novel.

Dave: It gained an incredible cult stature within the book industry. Almost immediately, it seemed to be the underground title everyone was talking about.
Whitehead: It's strange, really. It was a first book, you know? Any notice whatsoever I thought was great. It was in bookstores! But I thought it was too bizarre an idea. Maybe some weird freaks would be into it, right?

The sci-fi people latched onto it first, when no one had read it yet and people were just going by reviews. Then I read for audiences, and it was a really broad spectrum of people who showed up. It was a young audience in some places, then in others I'd have older crowds. It was strange how people came to it.

Dave: Do you think your audience will change at all with *John Henry Days*?
Whitehead: I'm not sure. It's great to see people that I recognize from earlier readings. Someone will ask a question, and I'll realize, "Oh, you came back!" It's totally nice. The crowds are larger, but the first book just came out two years ago so it's still reaching people. I don't know. It's strange. The readings are always really fun. The people come out—or sometimes they don't!—but you get to meet your readers, and they're the people you're writing for, not the interviewers or critics.

Also, I'm in my house all the time, and it's nice to get out, to tell you the truth—get some sun and fresh air.

Dave: You'd written half of *John Henry Days* before *The Intuitionist* was published. Now you're well into your third novel as the second one is hitting stores.
Whitehead: The production lagtime working with these big conglomerates is pretty long, so I had a whole year to write half of *John Henry Days* before *The Intuitionist* came out. Once I finished promoting that, things got back to normal, and I picked up where I'd left off.

In some ways it's irritating because you've finished a book, and you want it to come out the next day. But on the other hand, you're not stuck thinking, "What do I do next?" You're not totally lost like that because you've had the time to move forward.

Dave: Do you sweat much over individual sentences? It's not so much your vocabulary that's different, I think, but the way you use the words. All sorts of different verb usages, for instance. Familiar words in unfamiliar surroundings. It's active, and it reads fresh. Is that natural—are you just one lucky son-of-a-bitch, or is there a concerted effort to achieve that effect?

Whitehead: I'm not the kind of guy who spends an hour on a paragraph. I do hit-and-run revising: I'm bored, so I pick up a chapter and take out a word there, move a clause around. Over the course of six months I've slowly changed everything around to where I like it. There will be some chapters, when I'm copyediting, I'll be thinking, Oh, I really hate that chapter. I don't want to fix it, but I have to fix it. Then I look at it, and some time six weeks ago when I was bored I fixed it; it's done.

That works for me. People always talk about doing twenty drafts, but I do mini, drive-by drafts, I guess. By the end, I've revised a chapter twenty times, but piecemeal.

Dave: Is there any particular writing experience you're especially thankful for?

Whitehead: Being at the *Voice*, writing for different editors—there's a book editor and a music editor and so on—they all have things they like and don't like. You become aware that you do have readers with particular tastes. And they call you on your weaknesses, like, "Never use the word *infectious* in a music review." You become acutely aware of words you overuse, that kind of thing. the *Voice*, back in the day, was very hands-on editing. The editor would go through it, then you'd go through it together, so you see your mistakes in bold type. You become aware.

Also, you have immediate feedback. If you write a good piece, people will say, "Cool, man, I really liked the article!" And if you write a dud, no one says anything. Just deafening silence.

Dave: In reviews and articles, you're constantly compared to about eighteen other writers, some dead, some living. Do you read these writers whose names regularly appear in reviews of your books?

Whitehead: Jonathan Lethem has become a friend over the years. He blurbed my first book, and he compared it to Steven Millhauser. I thought, Uh oh! I've never heard of this guy!

Who do I read? It's sad, but I have a hard time reading fiction. I'm generally working on something, and I find fiction distracting. I read more nonfiction.

The people who influenced me a lot in college, when I first started reading the non-Dickens kind of Victorian novel of manners they foist on you in high school, were people like Ellison and Pynchon, stuff like that. Ishmael Reed. I like those guys, but they have a finite number of books, and I've read them. I like Richard Powers.

Basically, I like the kind of sprawling American books that talk about the culture. This year I met Myla Goldberg, so I got her book. I really liked it a lot. *Seabiscuit*, so . . .

Dave: What do you want to do now?
Whitehead: The other half of the novel. I'll write this play, and maybe someone will want to produce it. That would be a new kind of creative experience. It would get me out of the house and collaborating with people.

I feel pretty optimistic right now. But I'm superstitious, so I half-think that ten years from now I'll look back upon this conversation, pushing a mop somewhere, daydreaming about tattered clippings of good reviews.

I just want to try different things. Mix it up. I'm sure I'll try to do a non-fiction book in the future, but I'm not sure what. I'm not a good reporter, but I read somewhere that Joan Didion hates talking to people. She's really shy, so that's a great example of someone who doesn't like to talk to people but does. And it works out okay.

Dave: Why are you not a good reporter?
Whitehead: I've never mastered the art of the follow-up question. The few interviews I've done have been with musicians, five or six years ago, and I'd ask a question like, "Growing up, you must have listened to a lot of James Brown." "Yeah," the person will say. Well, I guess the logical next question is "How did it inform your musical choices later on?" But I'd just say, "Okay," and flip to the next question.

I have to work on those skills, I think.

Dave: In the interviews you've been giving to promote this new book, has anyone asked a question that's caught you off guard?

Whitehead: Someone asked, "Where do you and J. Sutter intersect and diverge?" I was like, "Uhhhh." I was stammering for a while.

Obviously, I have experiences in common with J., but I think he's an exaggeration of my worst qualities and entirely made up in a lot of different ways. But you're always like that: "It's not me!" You overprotest.

But it's not me, so just chill, you know?

Dave: "It's not me. Though I did see the film of John Henry in the fourth grade, it's true."
Whitehead: And I did work at the *Voice*. But there's nothing else! There's nothing else!

New Eclecticism: An Interview with Colson Whitehead

Linda Selzer / 2007

From *Callaloo* 31:2 (2008), 393–401. © 2008 Charles H. Rowell. Reprinted with permission from Johns Hopkins University Press. The following conversation between Colson White-head and Linda Selzer took place in October and November 2007.

Selzer: The innovative voice that you bring to American literature can be attributed in part to your familiarity with popular culture, from music and television to comic books and Internet cultures. I find it refreshing that even as your novels have achieved rapid recognition as "serious" literature, you have been open about your attraction to popular culture forms. Can you tell us a little about the pop culture that you find most interesting or important to you as a writer?

Whitehead: Anything I find interesting goes in the hopper and becomes an influence or inspiration to some degree. At various times, that's been comics, film, TV, music, and books—can't forget books! The things that made me want to write were things I read when I was little—*X-Men* and *Spider-Man* comics, then science fiction, horror, and fantasy novels. Who wouldn't want to write *Spider-Man*? It was a no-brainer. It wasn't until high school that I got exposed to Dostoyevsky and Dickens and started to think, Oh, a novel doesn't have to have werewolves to be interesting. Quite the revelation. And not until college when I started reading Ellison and Pynchon and Nathanael West, that I started to find a template for the kind of fiction I wanted to write. I think it's helped me that I don't see a distinction between the use of fantasy in, say, horror novels, and the use of fantastic elements in magical realism—the absurdity of Beckett, the surrealism of *Invisible Man*. The tweaked reality is a tool, and whether you use it for a low culture purpose or a high culture purpose is up to you.

Selzer: At the same time that popular culture provides an important inspiration for your work, your novels are often critical of what *John Henry Days* calls "Life under Pop." In fact, in that novel some of your most pointed satire is directed at the gangsta rappers whose blatant self-promotion skewers any notion that they can "keep it real" as their music becomes increasingly enmeshed in the designs of advertising culture. Did a sense of the limitations of pop forms lead you to begin writing what might be called serious fiction, or did something else motivate that transition?

Whitehead: Nonfiction and fiction are just two different ways of getting at the world. I grew up in New York City and was a big fan of the *Village Voice.* In high school and college it was my dream to be one of these interdisciplinary critics they had there at the time, merging the so-called high and low, talking about Derrida one day and Grandmaster Flash the next. Ah, youth. I was pretty excited when I started working for the *Voice*'s book section and began writing for different parts of the paper, but I knew I wanted to write fiction eventually. Writing for an audience, getting my voice down, and supporting myself by my work gave me the confidence to start writing fiction. The freelance lifestyle gave me the time I needed. I stopped writing nonfiction on a regular basis because I'd rather work on my books. I find it hard to switch between the two different modes, and since I'd rather write fiction, it seems like a waste of time to churn out articles. When I do take an assignment now, it's generally because I'm between projects or horribly bored or vaguely depressed, in which case it's a nice break.

Selzer: Since you mentioned Grandmaster Flash, I wonder if you might say a little more about your other interests in music. I know this might be an unmanageable question given your background in culture critique, but at one point in *John Henry Days* J. Sutter wishes that he could have been present at hip hop's neighborhood beginnings. What musical scene would you like to visit if given an opportunity? What music do you listen to when you are not listening to hip hop?

Whitehead: That would probably be CBGB in '75 or '76 to see Television (the band!), the Talking Heads, Suicide, and what not. Or *London Calling*–era Clash. As for what I listen to now, it's mostly electronic. Daft Punk, Hot Chip–type stuff. I play loud music when I'm working. That and the coffee keep me going. Because the new book takes place in the eighties, I've been revisiting people like Stetsasonic and Whodini, which is fun and low-tech and electronic in its way, but I don't listen to a lot of current hip hop.

Selzer: Did you make it to CBGB before the 2006 closing?
Whitehead: Yep, but '85 isn't '75.

Selzer: Somehow the interest in electronic music seems to fit. . . . Technology is important to your novels, and your narratives are alternately inflected by and suspicious of technological innovation. In *The Intuitionist* you describe the negative effects of the "first elevation" on the citizens of the city; in *John Henry Days* you write about a computer program, Office in a Box, which takes over the workplace to the extent that the virtual office replaces the physical workplace. In *Apex Hides the Hurt* you consider the effects of a media culture that runs the risk of reducing community to mere demographics. Would you like to elaborate on the issues generated by new technologies that particularly interest you?
Whitehead: Hmm—it's hard to elaborate because I said all I had to say about them in the books! If I could say it more concisely, I'd be writing pamphlets, I guess. I'm constitutionally leery of systems, whether we're talking about human organizations or new technologies. Every advancement has its benefits and its price. My outlook on the world prohibits me from cheerleading the latest thing—I always have to find the weakness, the hidden cost. So—the Intuitionists, despite their philosophy, have to be a bit corrupt as a group because they are human beings. The steam drill is more efficient, but what happens to the laborer? Apex, in superficially fixing one problem, creates others. And perhaps these other problems are entirely metaphorical, but they sure are worth exploring. I guess I wouldn't say I'm suspicious about new technologies specifically, but all sorts of things can go wrong when human beings get together—not to be too negative or anything. . . .

Selzer: Your novels have been associated with postmodernism, detective noir, black urban fiction, magical realism, image fiction, and post-soul aesthetics, and you have been compared to writers from Ellison to Doctorow, Morrison to DeLillo. Both *Apex Hides the Hurt* and *John Henry Days* warn about the dangers of branding or of assigning things to a category that effectively reduces them to a formula. Keeping the dangers of branding in mind, I wonder if you might still tell us a little about the literary genres, traditions, or previous writers that you have found most useful as a writer—or simply most enjoyable as a reader.
Whitehead: Like I said, everything goes in the hopper. The narrative design of *John Henry Days* owes a bit to Altman's *Nashville*, which I saw as a kid but which somehow ended up staying with me as I discovered when

I rewatched it toward the end of writing that book. Sometimes it's overt; sometimes influence is subconscious—you saw it, read it, and it made sense in a way that stayed with you, even if you didn't process it. So, Nathanael West's *Day of the Locust*, for the way he explores the machinery of pop culture while grounding it in a human story. *Invisible Man*, for the way Ellison balances a discussion of larger cultural issues and personal, existential questions in a narrative space that is alternately surreal and naturalistic. The *Amazing Spider-Man*, for giving me an early portrayal of the freelance life. Peter Parker is a stringer for a newspaper who lives in a crappy apartment and is always late with the rent. Classic. Richard Pryor and George Carlin, two social critics whom I encountered early on. *Ulysses. Moby Dick.* Edgar Lee Masters's *Spoon River Anthology* and Dos Passos's *USA Trilogy* for the unruly way they organize the world. I had to read *Spoon River* in my seventh-grade English class, and I don't know, it makes sense to me as a novel with a fractured structure. A lot of what passes for postmodernism is a repeat of what people have been doing for hundreds of years, so we should just call it all writing and be done with labels. Jean Toomer was a madman. Pynchon and DeLillo. Toni Morrison. Beckett and Eugene O'Neill. There's probably a bit of *Cooley High* in my new book.

Selzer: Now that you've mentioned *Nashville* and *Cooley High* I want to ask about other films that have stayed with you.

Whitehead: Eighty percent of Kubrick. I admire the tonal shifts between his movies, the various genres he tackles. It's inspiring. Zombie movies— Romero's *Living Dead* series with its strong black protagonists trying to keep ahead of the white living dead. The feel-bad movies from the seventies that everyone likes, especially those with a conspiracy angle—*The Conversation, The Parallax View*. What's not to love about *Citizen Kane*? Or seventies Scorsese?

Selzer: It's interesting to see that you mention Kubrick's tonal shifts and genre switching, and movies with conspiracy theories, all of which play a role in your fiction. I think that those who see connections between your writing and postmodernism are thinking about your work's narrative reflexivity—part of that self-conscious "tweaking of reality" you mention earlier— and the way that your writing challenges older conceptions of identity. I have to admit that *Apex Hides the Hurt* and *John Henry Days*, and to a lesser degree, *The Intuitionist*, call to my mind Baudrillard's analyses of branding and hyperreality. And your ability to take textual space across media boundaries makes me think of Barthes's work on image, music, and text. Are there particular critical schools or forms of culture critique that you've found particularly stimulating to you as a writer?

Whitehead: Short answer, no. Literary theory is great for discussing literature but hasn't been much help in writing the stuff. I didn't read any theory in college. It was only when I started working in the *Voice*'s book section that I started to dip a toe in. It was the start of the cultural studies boom, which we covered a lot, and a lot of our writers were academics. So I got a lot of second-hand lit-crit radiation. I felt I had to bone up on it so I could sound smart. The idea that it was okay to talk about pop culture in a serious way jibed with my own feelings about it, so it was nice to see people think seriously about music or TV, even if I didn't know what a lot of their words meant, especially the ones in italics. Are we living in a Society of the Spectacle? Sure—I saw *Network* when I was a kid so that phrase seemed to make sense. Even if I never did read Debord. I never read Baudrillard, but I read enough people talking about Baudrillard that I feel I got the gist. Or maybe I didn't. It doesn't actually matter. Certainly in my day-to-day writing life now, I don't think about theory that much. It's another element floating around in my brain that may or may not feed into what I'm working on next.

Selzer: I like the phrase "second-hand lit-crit radiation." Clearly your exposure hasn't been fatal. Your work does, though, consider questions about identity from a perspective within an information age that is increasingly governed by signs, one where consumption is keyed to brands and advertising rather than to the properties of things. At one point in *John Henry Days* J. Sutter suggests that he's too old to believe that there's "anything but publicity." That sentiment suggests a certain skepticism about the ability of words adequately to represent identity or experience. Do you share such skepticism? How would you characterize the current work environment for writers?

Whitehead: The situation is always hopeless, but we don't have any other choice but to do what we do: Write. If we could do anything else, we would. You know the litany. Bad art achieves success. Good art goes overlooked. No one reads anymore. People are spending too much time on the Internet. The chain stores kill the independent stores. The publishing industry is too white. People only want to read trash. Independent publishing is dead. It's always terrible. But we have no choice. And if the whole world suddenly worshipped ambitious writing, we'd still have the problem of filling the next blank page.

Selzer: Filling the next blank page. . . . Do you have particular strategies for dealing with that problem? Given the fact that you've produced three powerful novels and a prose collection in less than ten years, most people would categorize you as a prolific writer. I certainly would.

Whitehead: Things go best when I have another project to start thinking about when I finish something. Then when the self-loathing over not working sets in, I have something to jump into. And when I'm working, I'm fairly productive. I set a quota of pages for a week and try to meet it. If that means I work a lot on Monday and Tuesday, then skip the next couple of days and work on Sunday, that's okay. But I try to keep going—and when I'm between books, try to do nothing at all and recharge.

Selzer: Your list includes the observation that the publishing industry is too white. One kind of identity that you probe in your writing is black identity. In *Apex Hides the Hurt,* the nomenclature consultant who chooses names for various products comes up with the name "Apex" for a brand of multicultural adhesive bandages that are produced in a variety of skin colors. Because the bandages are poorly made, the novel seems to mount a critique of a sort of easy multicultural pluralism—identifying it as a quick patch for racial tensions. As the title suggests, they don't heal but only "hide the hurt." Do you find that multicultural diversity has been marketed in such a way that it's patching over significant problems?

Whitehead: Certain forms of multicultural cheerleading are as susceptible to corruption as capitalist boosterism and frontier idealism, two other systems I talk about in *Apex.* Every -ism has its weakness. Ideology, philosophy can transform and transport us. I think I was trying to explore what various systems can't do, as opposed to what they can do. *Apex* isn't the only Band-Aid in the book.

Selzer: The main character in *Apex* finally resolves the problem of what to name the town that has hired his nomenclature services. The fact that he arrives at a name suggests to me that he becomes more hopeful about the ability of words to push through the hype and to uncover the hurt. Is some recuperation of the force of words to represent experience, especially racial experience, suggested here?

Whitehead: That sounds almost hopeful. There's probably evidence to back up that hope. Also evidence in the book that undercuts it. In my own life, I try to hope that the world will improve, that various things will get better. Whether or not I put that in my books is a different matter.

Selzer: You clearly like to leave things open-ended—just as you do in the conclusions to your novels, which is one of the attractions of your fiction. Let me ask you about your creative nonfiction book, *The Colossus of New York*. In the first sentence of that collection one of the multiple narrators says that because he was born in New York he was "ruined for anywhere else." Is that pretty much the same reason why you moved back from your brief relocation to the West Coast?

Whitehead: If I could live anywhere else, I would. When I think of nice places to move, it's always a big city that comes to mind—London, Los Angeles. When I leave New York, I miss the misery. I miss twenty-four-hour bodegas. I don't drive, so I miss cabs. This is my home.

I started writing *Colossus* as a side project. I didn't know the pieces were a book—I was just having fun playing with the form and enjoying having a side project. After 9-11 they became more vital to me, as I tried to figure out how to live in a place that had been so injured, as I tried to figure out my own injury.

Selzer: That sounds like an ongoing process. You've written compellingly about what it was like to be in the city on that day. As you look back now from several years' distance, what stands out to you the most?

Whitehead: That I don't freak out every September, like I used to. It's probably too soon to have any perspective on it. I'm glad I'm here.

Selzer: Amen. . . . You mention that in writing *Colossus* you were having fun playing with its form. The narrative technique of that book is especially striking.

Whitehead: The narrative voice in *Colossus* comes from the country fair chapter in *John Henry Days*. In that chapter, I was trying to link the Talcott, West Virginia, fair with all fairs, in all towns—what are the universal experiences that define such an occasion, the mood and sound and smells, no matter where it takes place. I had a lot of fun with that voice and started using it to make impressionistic portraits of key New York places and states of being, Times Square and rush hour, the Brooklyn Bridge and Downtown, capturing a metropolitan feeling that is true for all cities, not just New York. Hopefully, you can apply your own feelings about your hometown to it. Faced with the lack of a main character or story I was following, the voice had to do the work, its rhythms. It telescopes out for a wide shot, zooms in for a closeup, details an abstract thought and then captures a small and concrete detail. And that back and forth makes a certain rhythm that pulls you along through each chapter. It is intended to be a chorus of citizens.

Selzer: So far your work has offered readers four distinctive narrative forms—the alternating narrators of *Colossus*; the surreal, almost solipsistic narrative space of *The Intuitionist*; the expansive canvas of *John Henry Days* with its multiple settings and time frames; and the condensed, formal elegance of *Apex Hides the Hurt*. Each is so different that you have me wondering, What's next?

Whitehead: Well, I try to do something different each time. If you know how to do something, why do it again? It's boring. My next book is about a group of teenagers growing up in Long Island in the 1980s. There are no weird subcultures, no big cultural theories, not much going on except what happens to these kids over the course of a summer. It's quite refreshing!

Selzer: It sounds like it may be the most realistic of your novels.

Whitehead: I think *Waiting for Godot* is high realism, so I'm probably the wrong person to judge that! But it's certainly linear and more conventional in terms of subject matter, so maybe that's realism.

Selzer: Would you mind sharing the title of the book?

Whitehead: It's called *Sag Harbor* and is slated for publication in 2009.

Selzer: I'm looking forward to reading that book. Thank you, Colson.

Marie Mockett Interviews Colson Whitehead

Marie Mockett / 2009

From *maudnewton.com* (April 29, 2009). © Marie Mutsuki Mockett. Reprinted with permission.

Colson Whitehead can subvert expectations with a single sentence. When Maud [Newton] asked me to interview him in conjunction with the publication of his marvelous new book, *Sag Harbor*, I was excited. I've been a fan since I stayed up all night devouring *The Intuitionist* years ago, but I also prepared myself for the unexpected (as you will understand once you click on the *Silence of the Lambs* Lego opera link he sent to me).

With *Sag Harbor*, Whitehead leaves the surreal and abstract worlds of *The Intuitionist* and *Apex Hides the Hurt* for a vividly captured summer of 1985 on the very grounded Long Island. *Sag Harbor* is hysterically funny, as Whitehead's novels have always been, with plenty of observations about popular culture and race, and scathing social commentary. Benji (or Ben, as he would prefer to be called) is an upper-middle-class African American fifteen-year-old caught between multiple worlds, including the delicate boundary between childhood and adulthood. He's old enough to wonder about his sister's absence from family gatherings but young enough to make sure he has mastered the lingo of his peers. "You could also preface things with a throat-clearing 'You fuckin', as in 'You fuckin' Cha-Ka from *Land of the Lost*-lookin' motherfucker', directed at Bobby, for example, who had light brown skin, light brown hair and indeed shared these characteristics with the hominid sidekick on the Saturday morning adventure show *Land of the Lost*."

With each page of *Sag Harbor*, I marveled over his virtuosic prose and deadly wit. But Whitehead is a serious artist, and the story is not purely a light and airy read. While he has always demonstrated compassion for his oftentimes isolated characters, *Sag Harbor* is infused with the anxiety of adolescence and a new warmth wrought from nostalgia.

Marie Mockett: An *Esquire* review of *Sag Harbor* contained this line about your work: "He seems post-conflicted, awfully comfy in whatever skin he's in." Is the adult Benji, looking back on his teenage years, post-conflicted? How do you feel about people wanting you to stand as an author who works out conflict for them? (Note: the reviewer did say he is jealous of you).

Colson Whitehead: The *Esquire* writer was a bit weird, since he seemed to be reviewing his idea of my persona, as opposed to the book. It was a bit too "it puts the lotion on itself for me." (Have you seen this: http://slog. thestranger.com/slog/archives/2009/04/07/put-the-fucking-poodle-in-the-basket, by the way?) I'm the coolest writer in America?—I spend 95 percent of my time in my house padding around in pajamas covered in dried minestrone. (The coolest writer in America is obviously Mr. Freeze, DC Comics villain and author of the memoir *Early On I Made a Decision to Incorporate a Cold Motif into My Crime Sprees: A Life*). Of course Benji is conflicted, confused, disassociating, plodding along. To confuse his adult self's ordering of his teenage self's experience with "post-conflicted" is a bit dense.

MM: In rereading your other novels, I was reminded once more of how deftly you handle the subject of race. *The Intuitionist* can be enjoyed as a slightly disturbing mystery with a sly sense of humor; it can also be read as an allegory. *Apex Hides the Hurt* has this fascinating abstract quality to it and is terrifically funny; it is also, as you have said, about race. Were you consciously aware while writing that your novels work on a variety of levels, and did you intend for them to work this way?

CW: I can't say if how I present my pet preoccupations—race, the City, pop culture, waffle cones—make it easier for people to relate to, or inhabit, my stories. Generally, the metaphors evolve over the course of the planning and writing of the book. I didn't know I was going to be able to tease out so much about race and architecture when I started *The Intuitionist*—the symbols and rhetoric revealed themselves the further I got into the book. And once you figure out a new aspect, that leads you to another, and so on. As for the allegory/fabulist tale/parable part—I grew up on comics and sci-fi, so the tweaked/heightened/absurdified/mythologized rendering of reality is part of the toolkit from way back.

MM: In a *New York Magazine* interview, conducted when you were still drafting *Sag Harbor*, you are quoted as saying, "I'm still trying to figure out how to write about stuff that's more directly from my experience." Is this something that you want to be able to do or feel you should do, and if so, why?

CW: So long ago. Looking back at my notes, I was only four—a whopping four—pages into the book, so I'd say, yes, I was definitely still figuring out how *Sag Harbor* was going to work. Do you have to figure out how to use stuff that comes directly from your life? No. If you want to write *GilagaTech: The Robot Chronicles*, a seven-volume (projected) series about a race of warrior robots and the spunky human child who leads them, and there's nothing from your everyday in it, go for it. It depends on what you're working on. For this book, definitely—I had a set of disorganized life experiences and needed to discover how to shape, spindle, and mutilate them into an interesting story. Drab piece of cheap bond manipulated into gorgeous origami crane, that's my motto.

MM: The parents in *Sag Harbor* make brief but pretty memorable appearances. Benji's father comes across as particularly forbidding. How did you go about shaping the father character, and did you feel sympathy for him? Do you empathize more with the father's background than Benji is able to?
CW: I have a hard time figuring out how much empathy Benji has for his father and mother, as I see him as in so much denial about the larger family forces around him. I didn't want him to process; it takes years and years to understand what's going on around us in our houses, and I wanted to depict that. (Hence no tidy resolution on Labor Day; life is not that neat.) Did I feel sympathy for the father? At the end of the day, they're constructs. When I read back over stuff I've written, I have a more sentimental response, based on the day-to-day progress: I remember when I figured out the sister's cameo; I went out and had a good steak. God, it was hot when I wrote the Afro scene; I was listening to Jay Reatard and sweating like a pig.

MM: Are you surprised by the ways people from all backgrounds see themselves in your fiction and respond to your characters, and how does it make you feel? Or are you used to this by now?
CW: I'd have a very narrow audience if it consisted of skinny black guys from Manhattan, not that we don't buy books. We do. Occasionally. It makes me very happy that anyone wants to read my books, and it's kind of the point to make that big bad Other of everyone else understand what you're trying to do. I do find it a bit strange when people say, "I'm a fifty-five-year-old lady lumberjack, and I could relate to your story." Do you only read books by fifty-five-year-old lady lumberjacks? Why are you so surprised?

MM: You've mentioned that prior to *Sag Harbor*, your protagonists have been writers in one form or another. In *Apex Hides the Hurt*, you describe the nameless nomenclature consultant's process: "He pictured it like this: The door opened up on a magnificent and secret landscape. His interior. He clambered over rocks and mountain ranges composed of odd and alien minerals, he stepped around strange flora, saplings that curtsied eccentrically, low shrubs that extended bizarre fronds. This unreckoned land of his possessed colors he had never seen before." This is the sort of passage that makes me feel that you have tremendous empathy for your characters, even as some critics have called you detached. As for the passage above, is writing ever this emotional and acid trip–like for you?

CW: There, I'm trying to describe what writing is like, as well as in the opening inspection/bribery scene in *The Intuitionist,* and in Lucien's bizarre PR meditations in *John Henry Days.* But you're using the thing to describe the thing itself—which is probably very complicated according to some school of philosophy or critical discourse that is over my head and anyway I'm too old for new tricks—so you can only fail. Is Benji a writer? I don't know.

MM: I have this impression that your mind works very quickly and that perfect sentences and deadly phrases just roll out of you fully formed. Your Twitter feed, for example, seems effortless and precise. How much tinkering do you have to do on a sentence level as you edit, or do lines and observations like this come out of you in perfect shape?

CW: You know—sometimes they come out right the first time, but usually they take years to get right, which is why it's good that novels take years to write. You have some time to work on them. If there's something I don't understand how to do—fix a sentence or get a character's voice down—I'll wait. Eventually I'll get it—I have to because I can't hand the book in until I do. "He stood" generally comes out perfect. "He leapt to his feet and ejaculated, 'We'll do it for Joey!'" can take years before it is transformed into "He stood."

MM: Has having a child changed your writing habits?

CW: Things were fine until she learned to walk. Then she started barging in with "Daddy!" and that's so beautiful that it's hard to pretend that getting back to work is important. But I didn't work for two years, and I had to get an office. Now that she's in school, I have the house to myself again. If only I had something to work on.

Who We Are Now: A Conversation with Colson Whitehead

Jeremiah Chamberlin / 2009

From *Fiction Writers Review*, May 30, 2009. Reprinted with permission of Jeremiah Chamberlin.

Jeremiah Chamberlin: Let's begin before the book. Some authors describe the writing process as a kind of possession—they hear the first line or a character's voice, and it leads them into the story. Others think of it more like exploration. Salvatore Scibona, for example, related in a recent interview that he began writing *The End* to describe the sound of a man's footsteps on a stairway, and then what might follow—the top of the stairs? A door? Was there a voice or an image or an artifact that brought you into *Sag Harbor*?

Colson Whitehead: I lost all my vinyl in a basement flood a couple years ago, so I had to go back and get all this old stuff (hip hop and the new wave and postpunk). And each time I remembered some old artist I remembered more and more of the eighties. So for me, I was consciously looking out for artifacts of the time—new Coke, old Coke, certain songs, certain TV shows—trying to find what would work for Benji's story and what wouldn't work.

JC: So there was already a story percolating as you accumulated these artifacts?

CW: I knew it was going to be the summer, and early on I decided on the summer of 1985. I wanted to write about Slick Rick and Doug E. Fresh and "La Di Da Di" and "The Show," this very monumental single that came out in the history of hip hop. It spoke to a time when hip hop was changing from a very juvenile form into a more mature one. So you had these corny singles and bands like U.T.F.O. (Untouchable Force Organization) and Whodini, and then eventually N.W.A. and gangster rap in the late 1980s.

I had also reconnected with Sag Harbor after fifteen years. I started going out there again, and each time I would bring friends out for the weekend I had to explain who this person was or whose house was that or what happened on this street. I was tied to the place in so many different ways, and there was a history of this black community that had to be told. So it was good material, and it was material that I knew very well. But I couldn't get to it. I had to finish *Apex Hides the Hurt*.

Then my daughter was born, and two years passed before I was finally able to start working on it full-time. But very quickly I knew that I wasn't going to have artificial coming of age events like a lynching or a big fire or someone accidentally killed. So I did spend a lot of the time when I wasn't writing thinking about how to elevate these very mundane moments into the stuff that was art worthy. I started making notes like, *Go to the beach? Get a summer job?* And then I had to ask myself, "How do these small events eventually become chapters, become compelling points of intrigue for the reader?"

JC: Zadie Smith once said she felt there were two types of novelists: the macro planner and the micro manager. She said, "You will recognize a macro planner from his Post-its, from those Moleskines he insists on buying. A macro planner takes notes, organizes material, configures a plot, and creates a structure—all before he writes the title page." Whereas micro managers, like herself, "start at the first sentence of a novel and . . . finish at the last." For example, it took her nearly two years to write the first twenty pages of *On Beauty* because she was trying to establish the right voice and point-of-view to begin the book. But then, once she had that in place, she was able to complete the rest of the novel in five months. Your process sounds more like the former.

CW: I always outline and have a pretty solid idea of beginning, middle, and end, though this can change over time. In my previous books, if I got sick of a character I could jump to a different section and work on that. So for the first time I didn't skip around. But, again, I had a few years of not-very-dedicated taking notes where I could write two lines about, say, "Should I name the character NP?" Then that would be it for one month. Basically, it was an ebb and flow of working on the book and taking notes.

JC: But you had a vision of the broad architecture.

CW: Yeah. Both things come at once—the voice of the narrator and how the characters talk and also the larger structure. To jump off your Zadie Smith example, I *am* sort of casting about for the first fifty or seventy pages as I finally nail down the voice. At that point I might go back and smooth out the early parts that aren't in that voice. The first hard part to get through is finding the voice, and then also setting the stage. I always find introducing the characters—are they tall, short, blah, blah; Sag Harbor's a town that was founded in blah, blah—irritating. So I really like it when I can let it rip. In this book, the first two chapters are setting the stage, introducing the players. But I had a lot more fun writing once I could let Benji have free rein.

JC: What I liked most about the narrative voice is your blend of the adult retrospective and the vernacular of this period, which helps capture the personality of Benji as a boy. Was that something that you had to work on?

CW: Before I started writing, I knew that it had to be an adult looking back on his childhood because I would get bored out of my skull if I had to have a fifteen-year-old's voice for three hundred pages. I know people fudge it by having very precocious narrators who are wise beyond their years, but that feels like a real cheat. I was not a very articulate fifteen-year-old, so why pretend that fifteen-year-olds are incredibly articulate and wise about their world? My narrators generally have a certain kind of critical faculty. They're analyzing what the characters are doing in larger social structures, so I wanted to have an adult voice looking back upon teenage years with that kind of critical distance—you know, being able to break down their cursing grammar.

JC: Yeah, I love the graph. [*Both laugh*]

CW: What I like about writing is the superzoom-in, and getting close on some sort of mundane thing, like frozen food or Classic Coke. My idea of a fifteen-year-old couldn't have that kind of critical voice in the same way.

JC: You mentioned the historical side of this black community in Sag Harbor earlier. Did you ever consider tackling this subject as nonfiction?

CW: No. [*laughs*] I'm not sure, outside of two pages, what the story is in a journalistic sense. I mean, they came in the thirties, started hanging out there, and . . . that's the story. Perhaps there is an interesting story about my grandparents' generation and their ideas of the world and what it means to be American and a black American and what it meant to achieve, to be part of this new emergent black middle class, and to have this place. However, I wouldn't want to spend two years talking to the old timers. [*laughs*] Someone else can do that.

JC: I was just curious because so much of the book has this interesting idea about legacy and what we inherit.

CW: Yes.

JC: Benji seems very interested in what he should know versus what he does know, and that's involved with the theme of identity creation woven throughout the book. The thing that I also found interesting, though, which we see during the picnic when he's watching the footrace and observing both the kids and adults around him, is that while part of identity creation is a very active process, another part of it seems totally out of one's hands, that there are roles we fit into.

CW: Well, nature or nurture, right? There are cultural codes, teenage codes, and social cues you pick up and learn to be a functional member of society, not ostracized and humiliated constantly. And that's the conflict between our idea of self and the way people are accepted into the larger community. Then there's this idea that we are all pretty much alike—the kid with the scabby knees and the messed-up haircut is us at some point; the older, middle-aged guy holding his Budweiser on his paunch is us in the future; and then we're going to be this oldster looking down upon our previous selves with a certain kind of bemusement, a kind of acceptance of the time traveler's paradox. Because you can't actually go back and fix your past, you can't go give your earlier self advice and have it move through things. You have to experience it yourself. In that way we're not individuals. We are part of this essential human being who is always learning and is always being replaced by some better version or older version—hopefully a more mature version—that is taking the place of who we are now.

It's saying goodbye. But I think particularly with Benji there's this hope that one day he will be on the sidelines of the race with his wife and his kid, that he will find himself. He's campaigning to become Ben, and not necessarily getting results, but at some point this campaign will have some sort of victory or success.

JC: The book also has so much to do with figuring out what nostalgia is, and how much of that's a manufactured process.

CW: Embracing the myth and realizing the myth is just that: a myth.

JC: And then embrace it again.

CW: Yeah, exactly. But it's okay. Or forgetting. This constant forgetting that it is actually fake, and discovering that it's sort of false and then forgetting again, and getting caught up. This cycle of remembering and forgetting that it's fake.

JC: And that that's all right.

CW: Yeah, it's okay. [*laughs*]

JC: Speaking of adults and childhood, let's talk about the parents in this book. In Toure's *New York Times* review of *Sag Harbor*, the book is briefly described as a *Peanuts* world, absent of adults. Yet Benji's parents—to borrow a metaphor from the book—seem like the "undertow" of this novel. Would you talk about their role here?

CW: There's no strong plotline in the book, so how do you create tension, anticipation? Part of that is by withholding information and revealing it at a key time. So, a hundred pages go by and you're like, "Where are the parents? What's going on? What's the back-story of their disappearance? Why aren't they there?" It's explained in a simple way: they work in the city. But how does that play out over the weeks? From chapter to chapter I'm establishing and then gradually building tension around this greater darkness that is slowly revealing itself. So they (the parents) appear, disappear. The book is ordered so that moving forward, creating tension, dissipating tension, there's more humorous parts held up against more miserable parts. For example, what is the effect when you go from the barbecue-from-hell chapter to this junior spy caper about getting into a club?

JC: And what is that, for you?

CW: It's an attempt to get to how we live. We're all veering from the tragic and the blessed moments across the span of a day. *The Colossus of New York* is very preoccupied with that, going through people's heads from sentence to sentence. Some people are having a good day, and some people are having a bad day. And it can change over the course of a city block. You can be having a good day on 62nd Street, and by the time you get to 63rd something horrible has happened. Whether it's Beckett or Richard Pryor, artists who I liked growing up veer between the capricious horribleness of the everyday and the absurd beauty of existence. So for me the duality has always been important in terms of how I see the world, and I think that plays out in my fiction.

JC: It also goes back to the idea of grief and hope bumping up against each other, right?

CW: It's simultaneous, yeah.

JC: We've talked a lot about how this book came into being and was constructed, but I'd also be curious to know about some of the most joyful moments you had during the writing of this book. [*Colson laughs.*] It's a cheesy word, isn't it?

CW: No, no, it's true. That's how I feel about it. [*thoughtful pause*] When I think about the writing of the book, I have a very strong sense of where and what room I was in. Was I in Sag Harbor? Was I in Brooklyn? Was I on book tour? Was I on the train? I remember when I came up with different things, so my reaction to the book becomes very sentimental. Like, Oh, that was a rainy day, and I was really hungry. And I broke open my notebook, and I had a productive afternoon. And that was a good day.

I remember the week of the last chapter. I'd already written the first seven chapters, so the voice was down. I knew what I had to do. I knew the characters well, I knew what I wanted to say, and I'd been thinking about it on and off for four years so that chapter came very effortlessly. I was sad to be done, but there was something really nice about finally pulling all the threads together that I'd been working on.

JC: You've talked pretty openly about the fact that a large part of this book is autobiographical. What, then, was the greater project of the novel?
CW: With earlier novels, there were questions I wanted to explore from the outset: How do you update this industrial age from John Henry to the information age? Or, in *Apex Hides the Hurt*: What do names mean? What does it mean for a city to evolve over time? And how do we ascribe meaning to places with the faulty tool of language, which is already a mediated meaning? So with this one, I didn't have a set idea. I just wanted to describe a way of being in the world that hopefully overlapped with other people's ways of being in the world.

JC: Do you think that changed your process in writing this book compared to the others?
CW: When the writing slowed down it was because I was trying to figure out what I remembered from being a teenager, or what I had discovered about the time period and the community that would work in the story. In previous books, I had a lot more free rein to invent stuff. Some of them take place in very fantastic stages, or there's a kind of heightened reality. So I had to figure out how to play it straight and stick to the facts and make the facts useful in the story.

JC: There seem to be ways that the language shifts between your books, too. The prose of *John Henry Days*, for example, is chiseled in a very different way than the prose in *Sag Harbor*. Do you think that has more to do with your language evolving as a writer in general or, rather, the narrative differences in those novels?

CW: The narrative differences, yes, but also just maturing as a writer. Ben has a sort of voice, and I have to stick to that. With *John Henry Days* I wanted the narrator to bend to whatever situation or character he was narrating. So the J. Sutter chapters are very frenetic, very charged up. With the John Henry chapters, on the other hand, I wanted a different kind of prose—shorter sentences, fewer adjectives, shorter nouns. It's very direct. I was trying to use the right tool for the job. So it is both. Hopefully ten years later I'm just a better writer. If I did *John Henry Days* now it would look different because I'm interested in different things and write differently.

JC: A final question as we wrap up. Is there one thing that you've been happy to let go of in this process?

CW: This may change, but I feel comfortable with where I am in my career and in my home life. I'm not sure what I'm going to do next, but whatever it is, it's okay. I enjoy this book, which I'm very proud of, and I enjoy having done some good work. When the next thing presents itself, I'll get myself into it. But instead of beating myself up and getting on this treadmill and saying, "I have to prove to myself I can do this," or that I have to do a big book or a small book, I feel my books have been different enough that I can chill for now. This month, anyway. [*both laugh*]

JC: For the next thirty days, right?

CW: At least until June.

Colson Whitehead Interview

Corban Goble / 2009

From *Epilogue*, June 2009. Reprinted with permission from Corban Goble
for *Epilogue* magazine.

Epilogue: First of all, I'm sorry to hear about your cat. I read about that on Twitter.

Colson Whitehead: [*laughs*] Thanks. She was a good cat and had a nice, rewarding life, as much as we could tell.

E: Why was 2009 the right time to put out *Sag Harbor*?

CW: I started working on it four years ago, and I think in order to write about one's childhood or adolescence you need a little more distance. I had no interest in my twenties to write about being a teenager, and it took a good long while to have enough critical distance that I could shape the material into something worthy of a book. And also just the technical chops because I hadn't done a first-person narrator before for a whole book. I tried and it never really turned out the way I wanted it to. So it took me four or five books for me to understand how to make a first-person narrator, and it took a couple years to figure out how to write about adolescence, get those other things out of my system and come back to this material.

E: How do you stay well-rounded?

CW: I try not to be bored. In terms of books, I definitely try to make each book different than the one before in terms of subject and narrative style, so say *The Intuitionist* has a very strong linear plot, a parody of a detective novel, and has a main character who's very repressed and laconic. In order to have an antidote to that book, *John Henry Days* has a lot of different characters, it's very open, it sort of prowls the prairie, and it's very different in style and structure from *The Intuitionist*. So really I'm just trying not to do the same thing in order for me not to get bored and for people who follow my books not to get bored.

E: What's the landscape like for novelists?
CW: If you're starting off as a writer, what you always should have done is to just keep working to make the book the best that it can be. The level of the artist is always the same whether it's 1899 or 2009. How do you keep producing quality work, and how do you get it out there to people in an indifferent marketplace? It's very hard to put out a first novel now because of the convulsions of the publishing industry. I know people who had their first books come out this year, they're not really going on tour, and there are fewer venues for it to get reviewed in. With that said, it's always hard; it always will be hard. The only thing that changes it is the quality of terrible that you encounter when you put a book out.

E: I read *Sag Harbor* on my Kindle.
CW: It's not that people are going to stop making art; it's just how we receive it that's going to change. The Kindle is the death of the object, but it's not the death of art.

E: How do you think publishing will evolve?
CW: I don't know. I'm not sort of a . . . marketplace theoretician. . . . In terms of journalism, I never buy a paper magazine. I get it all online, and if it's not online I barely consider it to exist at all. And the problem is not having people pay for it or knowing how to monetize it . . . so, again going back to my earlier point, it's not like journalists are going to stop finding stories; it's just that the way we receive them is different. It's not like people aren't interested in the news; they just don't want to pay for the physical object.

E: There's more content demanded than ever.
CW: Yes. You know, I wouldn't read the *Washington Post* or the *San Francisco Chronicle* if they weren't online, but I do read them because I can get them. I'm reading more arts coverage, following arts and political blogs, so I'm actually getting a lot more kinds of information. But I'm not paying for it.

E: What kind of things do you read or listen to? What's the creative process for you like?
CW: When I'm between books I'm sort of reading nothing at all, just

around the house, surfing the web or reading or watching TV. When I'm working, I try to keep abreast, not abreast, but I always try to find new music—electronic, big beatbox stuff, which makes me excited. I just got the new Danger Mouse/Sparklehorse record. When I'm working, I put on a lot of loud music, from the Clash, Daft Punk, whatever . . . I know some people have to have a very quiet sanctum, but because I love very loudly I find it a very warm, conducive atmosphere. Growing up in the city, it's always loud. Whether it was a record or a siren going by or a jackhammer, I've had to work with sounds.

E: To what extent is *Sag Harbor* based on direct experience?
CW: Well, I can't give you a percentage. I grew up in New York, and I would go out to Sag Harbor in the summers. The environment, the atmosphere, it's all drawn from what I know about that place in the eighties. Certainly I'm not interesting enough . . . my '85 was not that interesting, so I had to make stuff up in order to get a novel out of it.

E: What kind of projects are you pursuing right now?
CW: I'm sort of between projects. I get way into a book if I have a book coming out, but I still don't know. And I'm fine with that. [*laughs*] Journalism is a side thing I do when I'm bored or have an idea. I have a few book ideas; I'm not sure which one I'm going to do . . . so I'll take the summer and relax, enjoy that the book's out, and start trying to figure things out come the fall.

E: What are the most important things you try to communicate about yourself?
CW: There's nothing offhand, you know . . . I have interests, and over the course of books they've crept into my work in small degrees or large degrees. I'm from New York, I like writing about New York, the city, where it's going, where it's been. Pop culture, race, technology . . . I can't say what kind of stuff I'll be doing in the future, but if I'm forced to point out the things that I've talked about, I'd point to those couple things. I don't have an agenda.

E: How do you feel about the good press surrounding your work?
CW: The critiques are specific to each book, and by the time the book is out, it's a little too late to go back and change it. The people who say they don't read reviews, I feel that they're always lying. I'm definitely curious until the first batch comes out . . . will people connect to it, understand it?

A good review is a good review and a bad review is a bad review. No matter what kind of reviews you get each day, the problem is the same: How do you create art? You can get some nice kudos or some condemnation, but the blank page is always waiting for you the next day. You're always alone the next day no matter how many things people said about you the day before.

E: Do you ever think about blogging? You're on Twitter . . .
CW: I feel like if I have creative energy it's best directed in my books or my articles. So blogging, I have a website. I put up news about the book or readings and stuff like that. In terms of Twittering, it's not something I would normally do, personality-wise, but since I am in between things I sort of like the outlet. I enjoy the randomness of it. I could stop tomorrow or a year or six months from now, but it's a nice random outlet in the middle of the day, which I've been enjoying.

An Interview with Colson Whitehead

Rob Spillman / 2009

First appeared in *Tin House* 10.4 (2009): 51–59. Reprinted with permission of *Tin House* magazine.

Colson Whitehead's novels *The Intuitionist, John Henry Days,* and *Apex Hides the Hurt* reveal a uniquely jazzy prose stylist with a prodigious gift for invention and a killer satirical instinct. Gliding beneath the seemingly placid surface of everyday life, Whitehead attacks issues of race, class, and consumerism like a shark in a smoking jacket. For this Whitehead has earned an array of honors, most notably the MacArthur "genius" grant. The interviewer has seen Whitehead use his intimidating bona fides at the poker table, where he has turned some of us at *Tin House* (who shall go nameless) into gibbering losers.

It can then come as a surprise that in person and away from the poker table Whitehead is quick to laugh and has a wicked sense of humor. At the 2007 Tin House Summer Writers Workshop, Whitehead gave a reading from his then novel-in-progress, *Sag Harbor,* in which he, complete with visual aids, gave an etymological breakdown of 1980s African American teenage put-downs. In *Sag Harbor,* which is set over the summer of 1985, Whitehead follows fifteen-year-old Benji, an awkward kid with a dad-inflicted bad haircut, as he moves from his swanky, mostly white high school to the universe of childhood friends who congregate in the buppie enclave of Sag Harbor, on the East End of Long Island neighboring the Hamptons, where he tries to assert his identity as he straddles black and white cultures, moving from roller disco bat mitzvahs to the cult of Adidas. The overtly autobiographical novel doesn't shy away from familiar demons of race, class, gentrification, and the enormous influence of pop culture in America. His first novel, *The Intuitionist,* published in 1999, took on the world of elevator inspectors and was followed by *John Henry Days* (2001), which dealt with the legacy of the man who battled the steam engine, and then *Apex Hides the Hurt* (2006), a look at the warped world of branding and the power of words to seduce, deceive, and comfort us. He has also written a collection of impressionistic essays, *The Colossus of New York* (2003), which can be read as a prose poem to his hometown. Before becoming a novelist, Whitehead was a culture critic for the *Village Voice*. The interview was conducted in a cafe near Whitehead's Brooklyn home.

Rob Spillman: Was there a Proustian madeleine moment that triggered the writing of *Sag Harbor*?
Colson Whitehead: Not really. At first my research was going to iTunes and downloading a lot of eighties music. And, bit by bit, I was re-creating mix tapes I had made twenty years before. The research was different because it was a lot of fun. I spent half the time thinking about it, staring off into space, and the whole summer would come back to me with these tiny little triggers.

RS: You mean aural triggers?
CW: Yeah.

RS: Was there any one song that brought it all back?
CW: Chapter six or seven is around [the band UTFO's song] "Roxanne, Roxanne." I went to YouTube and finding their old video with their crazy leather pants and haircuts and crappy production values brought back a certain flavor of 1984–85. My agent is British, and there is a lot of pop culture in the book. And she had no idea what I was talking about, so I sent her a lot of videos. I sent her "The Message" by Grandmaster Flash, which was shot in the bombed-out Bronx, and she said, "This is what I thought New York looked like when I moved here in 1995."

RS: You once said that your ideal reader would be you at the age of sixteen. What would your sixteen-year-old self think of *Sag Harbor*?
CW: When I was sixteen I hated reading anything about teenagers. I found the whole thing excruciating, so anything repeating what I was going through at the time I would have to reject. So I'm not sure my sixteen-year-old self could get through this book.

And I also had a strong dislike for boomer nostalgia. So I'm basically my own boomer talking about the eighties with a certain kind of sentimentality that I would have abhorred, that I did abhor. I'm not sure this book is for me.

RS: The parents in the novel are always talking to the kids about what they should know, tsk-tsking the things they don't know—Marcus Garvey, etc. . .
.

CW: Yeah, I just want to have fun.

RS: For me there is a clear moral through-line between your books regarding race, class, and materialism. In this way, are all of your novels autobiographical?

CW: Yeah. Whenever I'm bringing a new character on the stage, the early animating force comes from me. Whether it's protagonist, antagonist, I'm using stuff that I have felt to some degree, or people I feel empathy for. In this book, there is a more direct analog between the setup and my life that is more autobiographical. But if you ask me, I am in there in all of my work. And, strangely, I think *The Colossus of New York* is my most autobiographical book because there's no filter, there's no story I have to tell. It's just my impressions of living in the city without any sort of mediating structure or story I have to get across.

RS: Did you approach this novel in a different way than the others? Your previous novels have many layers, with numerous cultural references both high and low. You've said in the past that "everything gets thrown in the hopper"—with *Sag Harbor*, did you feel limited in anyway?

CW: Because I started as a culture critic for the *Voice*, writing music and TV reviews, and because pop music is so important to Benji and his friends, I was able to get my riffing in through the way they talk about music and pop culture of the time, so I did find that it was a relief not to have to invent a subculture. I didn't have to invent a slang for the junketeers or the elevator inspectors. It was really about re-creating teenage speech and thought patterns. So when I was stumped at the end of the day, it wasn't "How do these weirdoes see the world?" but more "How do I keep a through-line with Benji?"

RS: Do you think your years of writing first-person journalism at the *Village Voice* delayed your writing of an autobiographical novel?

CW: I think being superaware of what people my age were writing at the time prevented me from writing that autobiographical first novel or an overtly Gen-X-y first novel in 1996 or a novel about contemporary New York. My first job was opening packages for the books department at the *Voice*. They got forty books a day, and it was my job to sort them. So I was painfully self-conscious of what people my age were supposed to put out, what publishers were publishing, and how they were received. So anything that was expected, I found excruciating.

I think, also, being older and more comfortable with myself, I felt it was okay to write about adolescence and to use a more direct approach to the events in my life. It isn't a cop-out. It is how you pull it off that's the most important thing.

RS: But did you set out to write against the grain of what the standard auto-biographical novel is expected to be?

CW: Sure. The ones I can really name are *A Separate Peace*, *The Catcher in the Rye*, Stephen King's *The Body*, and in the traditional coming-of-age story there is a *Big Event*—you find a body, a boy witnesses a lynching, the KKK is chasing you—and so I really wanted to be true to everyday experience, to the traditional route of the summer, which is you are .001 percent smarter than you were at the beginning of the summer, and you haven't had a big, life-changing moment or epiphany. It is more these small, incremental changes that add up to a new self over time. That creates its own set of problems: How do you make these small, every-day moments interesting? How do you make a fifteen-year-old interesting for three hundred pages when he is really just walking around being angst-y?

RS: You could read this almost as a collective novel, especially since you use the word "you" a lot at that beginning.

CW: I did want to capture a sense of the community, warts and all, and present him as part of this tradition, playing a role in this shifting array of generations. It isn't just his story but all of their collective stories. An early title for the book was *The Replacements*, so they are all replacing each other in this dance. Sort of like your Labor Day self is replacing your Memorial Day self, so this personal replacement is being enacted on the community at large.

RS: Are the characters in *Sag Harbor* like Tolstoy's in *War and Peace*—mash-ups of everyone he had ever known? Did you start with real characters in mind? Did you ever feel constricted by reality?

CW: I started with direct models, but each time they talked or moved or walked on stage, they did something different than the original model, then the story would play certain demands on them, and so they would have to change. Now I'm at the point where I know my characters much better than the original people. I spent three and a half years thinking about the summer of 1985 and only three months living it.

RS: Was this a fun book to write? If "fun" is a word you can use when you're putting together a novel.

CW: When you have a good day at work it is fun. There's a small wave of exhilaration when you put a few competent sentences together. This book was more fun because the structure allowed me to use a lot more jokes. I wasn't sure other people would find the jokes funny, but I was definitely laughing.

RS: In your previous books, there is a lot of dark humor, but in those it was more dark situations that were extended. In *Sag Harbor* there is a lot more stand-up, like the etymological breakdown of slang, that are laugh-out-loud funny. To me it seemed like you were having a lot of fun.

CW: With *The Intuitionist* I am confined by the character of the book and Lila Mae's disposition—she's sour and repressed, so she's not going to be cracking a lot of jokes. The character of Benji and the situations allowed me to have a lot more fun.

RS: You use humor almost like a Trojan horse, as a means to sneak in more serious subject matter. Like in *Sag Harbor*, where Benji's Dominican boss pats his hair, a scene which is very funny, but it is right on the edge of turning into a serious situation, an absurd scene with potentially profound ramifications.

CW: My first response to Beckett, as a college kid, I was responding to that dynamic. Growing up we were a big TV-watching family, and at age seven, eight, watching George Carlin and Richard Pryor, they would have these sudden movements from the comedic to the tragic, these sudden sharp turns; that's something I learned from them. And then it becomes a way of pacing things, the push and pull between the two modes, the way one cancels out the other. I was very conscious of pacing, of where the jokes fell, where the more gruesome stuff was coming in. How do you shift the mood, destabilize the reader, but also move things forward?

RS: Remember in the movie *The King of Comedy*, De Niro says, "You gotta kick 'em in the stomach when they're laughing."

CW: Yes, I agree.

RS: John Lydon, aka Johnny Rotten, with Public Image Ltd., sang "anger is an energy." And William Gass, when asked why he writes, replied, "I hate. A lot. Hard." Is anger an engine for you?

CW: Yeah. When I was writing *The Intuitionist*, I had previously written a novel that no one liked, I had twenty-five rejections, and I was so angry at Manhattan, where all of the publishers were. I was living in Brooklyn, and I would walk across the bridge to save money and shake my fist and say, "You can't break me." So the whole time I was really angry and I was writing a book about elevator inspectors, I was shooting myself in the foot even more than before. So that was a useful fuel for sitting down and writing that book. With this book, it is down low. It is definitely in there.

RS: In *Sag Harbor*, Benji says, "Black boys with beach houses. It could mess with your head sometimes, if you were the susceptible sort." This book is set in the summer of 1985. Do you think that by the time your daughter, to whom this book is dedicated, is fifteen, she will be dealing with the same issues?

CW: It'll be there, but I'm not sure what form it will take after four/eight years of Obama. It is all about authenticity. It takes all different forms. "I have a lot of money, so I'm not authentic." "I'm poor and I aspire, so that makes me inauthentic." "I'm part of the new immigrant class coming to America; there's Americanness and my own culture that are battling." With her generation, there is still going to be the common struggle of identity. "Who am I in the various cultural narratives of my community and the culture at large?" Lord knows she'll have her own problems, but hopefully they won't be the same as mine. At bottom it will be, "What does it mean to be a person at this time?"

RS: To ask a mundane question, how do you physically work? Computer, typewriter, longhand?

CW: Both. I take notes for months and months and months, getting the characters and the plot. "Chapter 2, Go to the beach, question mark." With this book, each time I started a chapter I would go through the three notebooks and transcribe it. There was a lot of organizing in notebooks, outlining, early character stuff. It isn't really in until it is on the computer, then I do a lot of revision.

RS: How much volition do your characters have? Do they fight you, or do you have control?

CW: I have it mapped out, but the story changes as I go along. With *John Henry Days*, I remember coming to a section and not knowing who the character was. The PR guy, I had to skip him, and a year later I figured out who he was and wrote his chapter. And once I did find his voice it was fun, and I let him do what he wanted to do. With this book, because it is a first-person novel and I'd never figured out how to do first-person for a whole book, once I had Benji's voice down, since everything was through his eyes, I didn't feel like the supporting characters could run amok; he was always keeping the action on track since he was in the center.

RS: For a lot of writers, the joy in writing comes in surprising yourself. With this novel, was it harder to surprise yourself?

CW: Because it doesn't have much of a plot, since it is a series of snapshots and vignettes of the summer, I was surprised by the end of a chapter by how much I was able to get in there, how much I was able to get out of so little.

RS: In *Sag Harbor*, there's a wonderful passage describing adolescence: "Keeping my eyes open, gathering data, more and more facts, because if I had enough information I might know how to be. Listening and watching, taking notes for something that might one day be a diagram for an invention, a working self with moving parts." This is also a perfect description for most writers I know. Do you still feel this way?

CW: Oh yeah, but for me the biggest thing that's happened to me is my daughter being born and realizing there is a whole other way of living that involves a third person and taking care of them and taking care of their hopes and dreams and progress, and it isn't completely selfish, getting up really early in the morning, with no sleep. You figure out how to be a better writer, person, parent. And once you figure it out they're in college.

RS: When Elissa [Schappell] interviewed Toni Morrison for the *Paris Review*, Morrison said that she does not want to be referred to as a black writer or a woman writer, but simply as an American writer. Is there any way for you to avoid these kinds of labels?

CW: The labels are by and for the people. When I was starting off I was very essentialist—I'm a black writer. I was very self-conscious about what a black writer was. Like, I wasn't going to write about a shack in the South, walking down the road with your messed-up shoes. There are certain clichés about black literature that I rebelled against. I also identified with Ishmael Reed and Ralph Ellison, and so I saw myself as wanting to live up to their example. Now I don't see that at all. I feel like I'm just a writer trying to figure out the next book. While I did identify myself as a black writer at the beginning of my "career," I think that was a holdover from growing up in the seventies with the nationalist idea of what my role was. I'm fine with whatever the first line of review says, i.e., "black writer," "African American writer." Do people still say, "Philip Roth, Jewish American writer?"

RS: You never hear "white writer" or "Caucasian writer."

CW: That's the nature of the review business. I have bigger fish to fry.

RS: When did you discover Ellison?

CW: In junior high. In a seventh-grade summer anthology, a collection of American short fiction. It was the first chapter of *Invisible Man*, the "battle royal" section. It was so new and startling. I had never encountered such rigorous metaphor work before. There's a blonde, and she has an American flag tattoo; they're wrestling for a gold coin on an electrified mat. I didn't read the whole book until college, but I remember being glad that there was another weirdo—a black weirdo—out there.

RS: When do you remember being conscious of wanting to be a writer?

CW: Sixth grade, seventh grade. Reading *Spider-Man*, *X-Men*, thinking that would be a good gig. Reading *Carrie*, by Stephen King, which has an interesting formal structure, flashing back and forward. There were newspaper clippings and inserts.

RS: And it has the theme of the outsider.

CW: Right. I remember liking the structure of *Carrie*, and the fact that you could write about, say, telekinesis or werewolves or vampires and keep it entertaining.

RS: Do you still retain that entertainment button?

CW: The stuff about the detective novel in *The Intuitionist*, I still have a love for it. I don't read a lot of science fiction or horror these days, but I have a lot of affection for the form. When I think of future projects, I often think of doing a riff on some aspect of fantasy fiction. There's nothing wrong with being entertaining. With the way I write, it would be fun to take an aspect of genre fiction and step on it, the way I stepped on detective fiction earlier.

RS: In *Sag Harbor*, Benji hides his love of the cheesy easy-listening radio station. Do you have any current guilty musical pleasures?

CW: I think they're all in the novel. I don't listen to "lite" FM, but there is that station, WLNG, in Sag Harbor, and they aggressively play these one-hit wonders. And you've heard them before. After a while, you listen and start thinking, This song makes a lot of sense. Burt Bacharach makes a lot of sense. It's embarrassing. All these naked, desperate declarations.

RS: My son wanted me to ask you if you play any video games.

CW: No, not anymore. As a kid I played a lot of computer games. I'm a dork, so I had to reject all of my Apple II Plus games. Since I'm basically home alone all day, once I start playing a game, I'll play it compulsively and things will be lost. Someone recommended *Spore*.

RS: My son is way into *Spore*.

CW: Maybe I'll take that on book tour for the downtime.

RS: I'm warning you—it's easy to get sucked in and disappear forever. Leave breadcrumbs.

An Interview with Colson Whitehead

Robbie Baden / 2010

From *Yemassee* 17.2 (2010): 8–16. Reprinted with permission of Robbie Baden.

Robbie Baden: How did your friends, family, enemies, anyone you knew from growing up respond to *Sag Harbor*?

Colson Whitehead: They liked it. I definitely didn't know how the community would take it or accept it, but the older generation were really excited that their community was being written about and immortalized. That's definitely part of the intention of the book: to capture this not-so-well-known part of town. In terms of my friends who I grew up with when I saw them last summer they hadn't read it. They were like, "I heard I'm in it . . . Congratulations." But they hadn't actually read it yet.

Baden: It's important to some people that this place and time and experience was put into literature?

Whitehead: Well, for my parents' generation it was rare, and they were this part of a new black middle class. So Sag Harbor is actually a not-so-common thing to have in your life. They're very proud that they worked for it and proud that it is now down on paper.

Baden: How did you feel about approaching this? Did you feel like you had to do it at some point? Did you feel cautious?

Whitehead: I didn't feel I needed to do it. But after the previous novels, it was a nice way to get out of a certain kind of idea-driven book, which I've been doing. I've avoided using personal material. I seemed to just know as a writer, even, it was time to go there.

Baden: I'd heard you mention before that you didn't want to start with that autobiographical novel. But now you feel it has helped you to grow as a writer to revisit what may be autobiographical?

Whitehead: Well, it's a cliché; everyone does their autobiographical first novel. So I was very self-conscious and didn't want to do the cliché thing you're supposed to do.

Baden: How did it become a moment that helped you grow as a writer?
Whitehead: I hadn't had a first-person narrator for a whole book before. I'd done it for a few chapters, but never for that long. So can I do that? Can I do a book that doesn't have a very strong structure, that's more anecdotal and relies more on the narrator's perceptions as opposed to a very strong A to B to Z plot? And then just writing about being a teenager, which I never thought I would find interesting—how to make that into something compelling to work on and for other people to read.

Baden: Do you feel now, moving on to work in the future, that you will stick to the autobiographical vein, or use it differently?
Whitehead: No, it's just that book. It served its purpose and the next book is different. Just as the book before was different than *Sag Harbor*.

Baden: Do you feel like you captured Sag Harbor pretty well—the whole if-the-city-burns-down-type thing, you can rebuild it from my novel like Joyce with *Ulysses*?
Whitehead: I took liberties with what happened in '85. I mean my '85 was very boring. My friends aren't as interesting. They don't serve up as well-executed dialogue as in the book. So, yeah, I took certain liberties. But one thing I didn't want to change was certain temporal markers—this song came out in '85. And also the layout of the town, I wanted to preserve it. Part of the fun was going back and trying to re-create what it was like in '85, but also being true to what's there now.

Baden: Is that place, 1985 Sag Harbor—is it lost? If you go back now, is Sag Harbor way different?
Whitehead: Yeah. I'm capturing these boys at a place where they're about to become men. Hair changing. Hip hop is changing, going from this very corny manifestation to late eighties hard gangster hip hop. And Sag Harbor's changing, so all these things parallel each other. Before '85 it's a very sleepy, kitschy whaling town, former whaling town, but the glitzy Hamptons arc starting to intrude. The club Bayside is one sign of that. But yeah, that sleepy mellow Main Street does not exist anymore. It's all very high-end restaurants, boutiques. So I wanted to capture, to preserve Sag Harbor in that moment.

Baden: I read somewhere that you'd be left alone with your brother at times at Sag Harbor, and your parents would be gone. It sounds like a dream. Even having grown up in the nineties that seems so odd, so impossible.

Whitehead: Like summer now, kids are overscheduled. And the Sag Harbor kids go out in the summer now or out for a weekend or for a month of camp, and they're wearing helmets, bike helmets. And they have chess camp or baseball camp. It's a lot different. You hear the cliché, "We didn't even lock our doors." I think a lot of places were like that. When my parents were away, the next-door neighbor was there. There were other parents—you know, a group of likeminded souls out to preserve the neighborhood and neighbor kids.

Baden: Is Sag Harbor any longer a black enclave?

Whitehead: The neighborhood, Azure Ashland/Sag Harbor Hills, is a part of Sag Harbor which is predominantly white. But it's a black neighborhood. And now that neighborhood, just in terms of how real estate works, is much more mixed and no longer like 95 percent black.

Baden: You write *Sag Harbor* in a different form than previous novels, and you mentioned how you looked to the detective novel form for *The Intuitionist*. How did you go about approaching an already-set form?

Whitehead: You know, it's there and you take what you can use. And then you reinvent what you can, so it's interesting and new. The characters and structure provide a way for me to have fun. So I take what's already there, and hopefully I'm making a new spin on a durable genre.

Baden: Do you find it liberating? Somehow you take a form that is there, but did you feel more free in your skills as a writer to go from there?

Whitehead: I didn't feel any allegiance to write a proper detective novel. I was free to do my own thing. And, you know, I always am, because it's my book. I'm not stuck with following a certain convention.

Baden: Did you approach any of your other novels similar to the way you did with *The Intuitionist*—going in your own way with a given form, a given genre?

Whitehead: Not that I can think of. I was consciously using a detective novel structure in *The Intuitionist*, and I was avoiding certain common conventions of the coming-of-age novel (in *Sag Harbor*). So I guess probably not.

Baden: It seems, when you approach the novel and a certain genre, you do your own thing. Do you feel that way when you approach history or such big issues as race—do you feel it's sort of a form that's there, whatever the discourse is about, and you go off on your own?

Whitehead: I think there are clichés when talking about race, and I want to avoid them. I think when you say "freedom," I just think I'm a writer, and I have my own perspective that I'm putting out there. And I don't have to follow someone else's idea of how you write a novel or how you approach a subject. I'm hoping that people will come to my books assuming that I am doing something different.

Baden: I'm fascinated with a playfulness, but a seriousness, with which you approach history or race. And you mentioned last night, in a reference to Pynchon, how you like to portray huge social structures while you can zoom in on a character. Can you talk a little bit more on that?

Whitehead: We're adrift in these large social structures, political structures, racial dynamics. We're prey to the historical moments of our time. So how do you pull back and depict these larger currents, if you have something to say about them? I use a lot of [this] in *The Intuitionist* and *John Henry Days* and *Apex Hides the Hurt*. But I also have a character who can be a vehicle, who's interesting, who can interact with these different currents and make a compelling story.

Baden: Reading through *The Intuitionist*, I formed this image of the Empiricists as these sweaty old white guys with Coke-bottle glasses, heavy starched shirts, a pen protector, and a long history of ulcers and sweat. This is such a funny image of, say, baby boomers, whereas the Intuitionists are new, younger renegade types. It's interesting how they seem to show a generational difference, as much as or more than a racial difference. And I also heard you mention somewhere that terms, such as terms to identify race, will fall off, and a new generation will arrive with new terms and names. So how does generational difference play in how you think about writing?

Whitehead: It doesn't. But, if that's part of what I'm working on, then I want to address it. So definitely in *Sag Harbor* there's the grandparents' generation that got there in the thirties, my parents' generation started getting their own places in the sixties, and there's mine and my daughter's. So generation plays out in *Sag Harbor*, doesn't really play out in *John Henry Days* directly. It's about what's appropriate to the book and what I'm trying to say.

Baden: You focus on names, like in *Apex Hides the Hurt* we have the naming of a town. So in one sense it seems the name is very important, but in another sense you're at liberty to choose these names. And it's again recalling that idea that a new generation will name itself. How do you feel about the power of naming? What is so important about names, words?

Whitehead: Well, it is power. How we name ourselves. How we're addressed. I think *Apex Hides the Hurt* is just a big stage for a discussion of how names are used, wielded, voided. To get to an essential nature is it possible to actually name something properly? Can we name our world? Can we name our world and fix it in place? The protagonist of *Apex Hides the Hurt* is negotiating different ways of naming and being named during the course of the book.

Baden: Did you find a historical precedent for the naming of the town in *Apex Hides the Hurt*?

Whitehead: I was thinking so much of a naming of a town. There were all-black towns in Oklahoma and the Midwest. Folks who were fleeing the South after the Civil War. So I took off from that. In terms of his job as a nomenclature consultant, I read an article about the naming of Prozac. How to find the right prefix, suffix arrangement of syllables so that people would think that Prozac would be the right pill for them. And I thought, Oh, that's a weird job. And then just from living in New York City, there's so many street names you see, and you know who they are, Remsen and Schermerhorn and Hoyt. At one point they were important, they were people of power. Two hundred years later they're just a name on a street. I was thinking about that sort of circulation of power and influence in the city. I know you can rename a crappy neighborhood "Sunshine Vista" and suddenly put up some condos; it's no longer a crappy neighborhood. It's a new place. So just from thinking about cities, eventually I linked the two—someone who names and then how naming tracks the movement of power through time.

Baden: Do you have any quirks as a writer? In the process of writing.

Whitehead: I think it's all quirks. I think we all have our special things we do. I'm obsessive about keeping on track for my weekly page count. Eight seems like a good number. If I do six one week, I beat myself up and have to do ten the next week. And of course the system fails, and I have to feel depressed until I get myself back on track. I think whatever you do, if it works you then just go with it. We're all just freaks in our writing room.

Baden: Do you feel it's a method or a certain discipline you have to follow, or do you feel like it changes from time to time?

Whitehead: Before my child was born, I had more time. When I'm not teaching, I have more time to write. If it's a book that—you know, *Sag Harbor* is a very colloquial book, very slangy, a lot of jokes. So each book's different, and definitely the way I write evolves. You have to adapt to making money. With *The Intuitionist* it was writing journalism, one article a week. Then trying to get back into "fiction head," and then going back into "nonfiction head."

Baden: Do you know of any other writer's method of writing that is just absolutely ridiculous? Makes you laugh?

Whitehead: Well, if it works for you, it works for you. I sort of have to know what I'm going to do each day. I can't imagine opening up a story and wondering, "Does a sheriff come in with a gun or does he go shopping?" For me, not knowing, being in the dark about what's happening in my book the next day seems ridiculous. But if that works for you, who am I to impugn your style?

Baden: Who are the best writers now? Who are you enjoying?

Whitehead: I don't rate folks. But I like my friends; I like Jonathan Lethem. We're both from New York, about the same age. I like hearing the description of what he's working on, and I'm often like, "You're doing that? That's crazy." That always works out great. One of the fun things about, I guess, being a writer is that you meet other writers; you meet them as a person. Then you read their books, and you have a different sort of relationship with them. When you get folks who you like as folks and as people and also love their work, that's always a nice thing. So—Junot Díaz, I like what he's doing in those two books. Best? You know, my tastes change, my interests change.

Baden: What's your favorite word?

Whitehead: I don't have a favorite word. But I do like *pylon*; I think it sounds nice. I like *apex*. Just the word *apex*. And more about the way they sound as opposed to the meanings.

Baden: I listened to you in an interview talking about naming your child. You and your wife argued about the name, and you said you like names that are short.

Whitehead: Yeah, Nina. My wife was very fond of certain names, and I was like, "Those are all stripper names." We're not going to go with Montana—sorry. You come together and find a name.

Baden: What do you think about all the lit mags out today?

Whitehead: I don't read many lit mags, just because I feel—I just don't get out.

Colson Whitehead on His New Zombie Novel, *Zone One*, Destroying New York, and Apocalyptic Capitalism

Alyssa Rosenberg / 2011

From *ThinkProgress*, October 17, 2011. Copyright Center for American Progress Action Fund. Reprinted with permission of the author.

The novelist Colson Whitehead isn't new to science fiction and speculative fiction—his 1999 debut novel, *The Intuitionist*, was set in a world of competing schools of elevator inspectors and the dream of an elevator that could take riders to a perfect society. But his new book, *Zone One*, on bookshelves today, is an elegiac tale of plague, zombie-hunters in New York, and the limitations of efforts to build new societies. It is the result of Whitehead's longstanding plans to write a monster novel. We spoke at New York Comic Con about choosing average narrators rather than heroic ones, making monsters sympathetic, and the persistence of corporate sponsorship in the apocalypse. This interview has been edited for clarity and length.

Alyssa Rosenberg: Why a zombie novel?
Colson Whitehead: People are wondering. It was reading comic books—and watching horror and science-fiction movies—reading H. P. Lovecraft that made me want to be a writer. I've never seen much of a division between so-called genre fiction and literary fiction. So when I went to college, I wanted to write werewolf novels. I remember applying to college and saying this to the interviewer, and he's like, "No, what do you really want to write?" And I was like, "Yeah, no." In retrospect, an elevator inspector novel obviously turned out not to be a bestseller. I knew that I would do a horror

novel, book seven or book eight. It turned out to be book six. And zombies, in particular, seeing *Night of the Living Dead* and *Dawn of the Dead* when I was nine or ten, too early to be that state-of-the-art makeup, the idea of zombie terror stayed with me.

I'm not prepared to talk about the larger social currents and why they're big now among twenty-somethings and teenagers. For me, the terror of zombies also covers *Invasion of the Body Snatchers*, the idea that your family and friends and neighbors and teachers could suddenly overnight become monsters, or reveal themselves as the monsters they've always been, that's sort of my bad, Freudian interpretation. And it's what brought my conception of the book to mind.

AR: In a lot of these zombie stories, the hero is someone who's really extraordinary, someone who's going to find the cure or lead the people to freedom. Mark Spitz, the nickname of the main character through whose eyes we're seeing the world, is sort of relentless about his averageness. I was wondering how deliberate that choice was to make him representative rather than aspirational?

CW: Yeah, there are the shambling dead; he's like shambling mediocrity. I think when I was conceiving of the book, I figured, if you're really high-functioning and really cognizant of what's going on, you'd jump off a building. And if you're a C or D person, you'd be killed off quickly. For me, the survivors are all mediocrities. He's like a mediocrity among mediocrities. I'm not sure what kind of person ought to be in an apocalypse. I'm sure I'd be cut down pretty quickly. But it seems that someone who has always muddled through in organized society, his inefficiency to succeed becomes, actually, a successful adaptation.

AR: He seems sort of cut off. You mention at one point that religion has become more prevalent since the disaster, but he's also sort of emotionally reserved. Does that make him more like us as the readers?

CW: I'm not sure. Later on, there's a discussion of what monsters mean. There's his interpretation of what monsters mean, and people seem to be latching on to those passages relating how he feels about the other survivors and monsters. So, I kind of have two protagonists.

AR: Is it fun to destroy New York?

CW: It's a devastated New York. The way *Zone One* works, it's kind of like Wall Street at 2 a.m. is Zone One. There's no one around. Everything's closed. It's nonresidential. And it's dead . . . Growing up here in the seventies, there was always an idea of a ruined New York. It's dirty, rubble is everywhere, and the vandals have taken over. So I think that's definitely in there. The films that I watched as a kid—*Escape from New York*, *The Warriors*, *Planet of the Apes*—you find out the whole time that New York is heading for a bruising and perhaps that bruising is already here.

AR: New York seems to have the seeds of destruction in it. A creative destruction, maybe, because the city keeps changing.
CW: We talk about Bloomberg and Giuliani and how they've transformed the city over the last fifteen years. The downturn's going to come. Whether it's next year or ten years from now, that expansion and contraction is part of the life of the city. Of course, I'm in Brooklyn now . . . there were progressive waves of immigration, it gets run down in the eighties and nineties, and now it's a superrehabbed brownstone wonderland. And then, it goes back and forth.

AR: We don't have a lot of information. There are all these myths about Nobel Prize–winners off working somewhere, but it's not a particularly omniscient perspective. Does that make things scarier? Or pace out the introduction of the world?
CW: The destruction in the *Road Warrior*, you can't really consciously explain the devastation. In the first *Night of the Living Dead*, there's a line or two about a satellite that fell down, and maybe there's radiation. And that's kind of thrown out afterwards, but we're in the world of horror. What's more important is the psychological landscape.

AR: There's also a winsomeness in the horror when Mark Spitz sees the faces of all the people that he knows in the zombies that he's killing.
CW: It's ultimately about this character trying to find a way to make it through the day without getting killed. And how does he process what's happened to him, and the world, and move on to the next stage, Buffalo, or the next refuge after this one falls. In terms of the humor or my personality, I've always been much more grim and the jokes start seeping in.

AR: I love Kaitlyn, part of Mark's team, and this horrible repetition that she's been student council secretary.
CW: In real life, Gary and Kaitlyn, I would hate them, but I actually do have some affection for them as characters and the family unit they make.

They're dissimilar, they're thrown together, and they have antagonistic personalities. But they are a family. We don't get a choice in real life, either. But in the apocalypse, you have a smaller pool of people.

AR: Gary and Kaitlyn both struck me as, if not keepers of the civilizational flame, existing institutions. Gary's excited by the idea of a patent. Kaitlyn's still clinging to who she was. I thought it was striking that there's that moment when you talk through some of the social experiments that happened, but you try to keep things as normal as possible.

CW: The systems of the postapocalyptic stress disorder are the general symptoms to getting up on Monday. You've lost some sleep. You can't eat. You're gaining weight. You're losing weight. People like Gary and Kaitlyn are still stragglers in their own way. They're still tied to their preexisting notions despite the apocalypse. I'm trying to explore where the borders are between skel and straggler and survivor. How different are they?

AR: There's a continuum of humanity. There's a tendency to assume that we'd move towards fascist organizations, that we'd trade freedom for security. But the novel seems to suggest that humans stay human.

CW: The gaudier the structure, the quicker it comes back. So marketing, corporate sponsorships, bureaucracy, bureaucratic incompetence—like, they don't cap off the top of the island. There are certain tropes about postapocalyptic stories, especially ones that go on for a couple years. "Oh, here's another refuge and its crazy rules! Oh, now we've got to escape!" And you go to the next one and the next one. And it's a critique of every institution being parodied, whether it's fascistic, utopian, countercultural. So for me, my satirical take is the crappier the existing institution now, the more quickly it will come back.

Colson Whitehead on Sandwiches, Bunker Songs, and the Zombie Apocalypse

Melissa Locker / 2011

From *The Hairpin*, November 22, 2011. Reprinted with permission of Melissa Locker.

There have been many books written, movies made, and graphic novels turned into television shows about the undead. Yet when novelist Colson Whitehead tackles the subject, it feels like no one else has noticed that an inevitable zombie apocalypse looms over us. (Don't worry, he knows that sounds really depressing.) In his new book *Zone One*, the remainders of humanity battle the walking dead in lower Manhattan, and so we talked him into battling the walking dead *or* spinning some tunes with us on Turntable. fm. Topics include: R. Kelly, Edith Piaf.

[Melissa Locker plays "Love Zone" by Billy Ocean.]

Melissa Locker: Hi!
Colson Whitehead: Hey there . . . let me get at a gander at this newfangled "technology."

ML: Yes, welcome to Turntable.fm. Make yourself comfortable. We can just listen to some Billy Ocean. I picked this song because, well, it has "zone" in the title and your book is called *Zone One*. Clever, right? Plus, Billy Ocean.
CW: Thanks! Early on, the book was called *Monster Movie*, since the direct antecedents are horror and sci-fi flicks, but once I named the downtown section, *Zone One* sounded dorky and sci-fi. Something about the word "zone," I guess.

[Colson Whitehead plays "Buffalo Gals" by Malcolm McLaren.]

CW: I take it you are hearing "Buffalo Gals"?

ML: I am hearing the song. It must have helped with promotion when the city started zoning everything during the Great Hurricane Evacuation of '11.
CW: I missed the hurricane, sadly. I missed the Brooklyn tornado, the earthquake . . . whenever I leave town all the good stuff happens.

ML: So if you stay in town, maybe we'll miss the zombie apocalypse?
CW: I like it here, but if I never get to leave NYC, then the world really has ended.

[Melissa Locker plays "Astro Zombies" by the Misfits.]

CW: I sense a theme . . .

ML: Oh you got that?
CW: Two weeks ago, my friend was in CVS in LA and saw [Glenn] Danzig. He took a picture of him—from the back. Black hair, bald spot. It coulda been him.

ML: He's been around lately. He had a meltdown in Austin. I think astro-zombies would be worse than regular zombies.

[Colson Whitehead plays "Eight Miles High" by Hüsker Dü.]

ML: I love this song.
CW: My favorite mix-tape from tenth grade had the Byrds version and this version back to back. I think I was trying to make a statement.

ML: To yourself?
CW: I only made mix-tapes for myself! Heh!

ML: I truly miss mix-tapes. Spotify just doesn't cut it. Do kids these days just send the boys they like Spotify playlists? But back to zombies, what do you think the chances are of an actual zombie Armageddon? Pop culture seems really convinced it's going to happen.

[Melissa Locker plays "Cudi Zone" by Kid Cudi.]

CW: Well . . . nostalgia is one of my signs of creeping zombie-ism, I think. Being stuck in particular grooves, unable to escape them. Robotic devotion to the past. Not that it's all bad, but—you asked about the Zombie Apocalypse, and I think that's one of the symptoms. Straggler signs.

ML: So we're doing it to ourselves? Nineties nostalgia is going to do us all in?
CW: What are the things that we do every day that may be indicators that we're a bit dead . . . or not quite alive.

ML: Not drinking enough coffee.
CW: My last two books were deeply about nostalgia and trapped by old ideas of ourselves. . . . The coffee helps, and the egg sandwiches, goddammit.

ML: I think it was Kelly Oxford who asked yesterday, "How much longer do we have to tweet?" which was kind of weirdly eye-opening. Are we going to do that forever? Or will it take a Zombie Apocalypse to get us to stop?
CW: I've see that a few times from people. Can we just call it a day? My TweetDeck filter is bursting with stuff I'm trying to keep out of my feed!

[Colson Whitehead plays "The Light Pours Out of Me (Live) (2009 Digital Remaster)" by Magazine.]

CW: I guess my idea is that we can't stop, won't stop . . . we'll just persist.

ML: Until something stops us. That song title has a lot of parentheses.
CW: I know! And we didn't mention Kid Cudi, whom I know nothing about. Is that a person or a band? At any rate I'll have to investigate.

ML: It's a person. He's great. I don't know if he's on Twitter though. So, what is the first record you'd throw at a zombie if it was coming at you?
CW: I wouldn't throw a record, that's terrible. I would start singing "La Vie en Rose" to try to calm it down. "Chill out, bud."

ML: Edith Piaf stops zombies? Someone should tell those guys on *The Walking Dead*.
CW: If they've heard the song before.

[Melissa Locker plays "She's Not There" by the Zombies.]

ML: So there's no universal song to soothe the soulless?
CW: A lot of regional differences, like "Do you like Sriracha?" and stuff.

ML: Oh, so you have to know your skel? Head to Waffle Houses in the South?
CW: I was glad to have a set piece in TGI Friday's in the book. I enjoyed the research.

ML: Did you get the endless lunch? Well, I guess you wouldn't if you knew the world was going to end.

[Colson Whitehead plays "Senses Working Overtime" by XTC.]

ML: Your musical selections seem like a near soundtrack to another one of your books, *Sag Harbor*.
CW: I've been stuck in an eighties groove since writing that book. I dug into various new wave and post-punk for atmosphere and never fully emerged—the straggler part of me.

ML: The songs are really good, though. So maybe it's not nostalgia, but just good musical taste? When did you start working on *Zone One*?
CW: Summer of 2009. I'd taken two years off from writing after finishing *Sag Harbor*, and the horror novel was the first thing that seemed compelling to work on.

[Melissa Locker plays "This Town Doesn't Have Enough Bars for Both of Us" by Gospel Music.]

CW: I handed it in last January, was editing all through the spring, so I never really had a postbook recuperation time. All I want to do now that the book is out is hang out on my couch and eat sandwiches.

ML: Sandwiches and couches are a good solution to most problems.
CW: Who are these characters singing?

ML: This is a guy named Owen Holmes. It's his first solo project. He goes by Gospel Music. He'll be in New York in December.

[Colson Whitehead plays "Scum" by Nick Cave and the Bad Seeds.]

ML: Do you have a new book percolating? Or are you just thinking about PB & J versus salami?

CW: I tend to work intensively . . . and then decompress intensively. It seems to work! Not thinking about any project at all.

ML: I love this song. Have you read Nick Cave's fiction?

CW: Had this song on a flexi disc . . . It always struck me as a nice monologue. I wish I could do it in karaoke!

ML: You could do this in karaoke? Also, flexi disc? Whoa.

CW: Dude, I have been doing this in the shower for years. (I'm weird.)

ML: This would put my go-to karaoke song of "Careless Whisper" to shame.

[Melissa Locker plays "Heroes" by David Bowie.

CW: I have a pact with Nick: he doesn't hear me sing, and I don't read his fiction. (I'm sure it's quite good.)

ML: I've only read *And the Ass Saw the Angel,* and it was good. But if you won't read Nick Cave, what will you read?

CW: Just joshing. I would read Vanilla Ice's memoir. Just the 1996–2005 years.

ML: I want to read R. Kelly's memoir, *Soula Coaster.*

CW: Is that what it's called?

ML: Yes!

CW: Was I. P. Daly the co-writer?

ML: I assume. Unfortunately, it got held up by the publisher until spring.

CW: Good survivors-in-the-bunker song, by the way. Everyone else is dead, just us left.

ML: What else is a good survivor-in-the-bunker song? Although I would think this song would inspire people to go make a run for it.

CW: I'd loosen those boards on the window and split, sure. I'd probably get eaten, but you have to go for it. Have you seen *Christiane F*?

ML: No. I've seen *Dead Snow*, though, and *The Road*. Is it like that?
CW: No, it's a cautionary tale of drugged out seventies Berlin youth. Great Bowie footage. And scenes of teens in trouble.

ML: Oh, nothing to do with people in a bunker.

[Colson Whitehead plays "I Believe" by Buzzcocks.]

CW: No zombies, just great campy degradation. This is also a take-a-stand song—solo against the world, but still standing, etc.

ML: Did you watch any zombie movies while you were writing?
CW: I watch *Night of the Living Dead* twice a year. I did not increase or decrease my frequency.

ML: Christmas and Easter?
CW: Exactly! I had to have little zombie film festivals to explain to my friends what I was doing. Some were like, "I hate zombie movies." Then I'd ask, "Which ones didn't you like?" And they'd say, "Um, never seen one."

ML: What films did you include in your film fest? Have you seen *Dead Set*, where the zombies invade the Big Brother house?
CW: *Night of the Living Dead*, the original *Dawn of the Living Dead*, *28 Days Later*—that's a good intro. Enjoyed *Dead Set* very much. Thrown in *Return of the Living Dead* and then *Escape from New York* and *Omega Man* for general apocalypse action.

ML: Whenever I try to leave New York City for the weekend, I feel like I'm in *Escape from New York*. Like, what do you mean the Tappan Zee and 95 are closed?
CW: Exactly. The apocalypse is all around us; we're just too stupid to see.

ML: Well, then, I'm going back to bed or, at least, going to go sit on the couch and eat sandwiches.
CW: Didn't mean to bum you out. Oh, wait, I did. That's why I wrote the book.

[Melissa Locker plays "Invincible (Theme from *The Legend of Billie Jean*)" by Pat Benatar.]

ML: How do you feel about ending the interview on this song?
CW: Seems okay!

ML: I think this would be a good bunker song, too.
CW: Yes, as you check the ammunition stores.

ML: Okay, off to go stockpile Cipro, sandwiches, and ammunition.

The Rumpus Interview
with Colson Whitehead

Nancy Smith / 2012

From *The Rumpus*, July 17, 2012. Reprinted with permission of Nancy Smith.

Zone One, a literary, postapocalyptic horror novel takes place in Manhattan shortly after a plague, which has turned half the population into the living dead (or skels as they are called in the book). The novel follows Everyman survivor Mark Spitz as he sweeps an area south of Canal Street, looking for straggling skels and wrestling with a world that has fallen to ruin. It's a cool, smart take on a genre that, while its popularity comes and goes, never seems to lose its relevance. *Zone One* was released in paperback this July, so I chatted with Colson about his books, the writing life, and, of course, zombies.

The Rumpus: I lived in New York for a few years, and shortly after I moved there a friend gave me your collection of essays, *The Colossus of New York*. It was this great introduction to the city. I remember being sort of overwhelmed by the mythology that surrounds New York, but that book feels really grounded in daily life. Can you talk a little about that book, and what the process of writing it was like?

Colson Whitehead: The mythology, yeah. I guess I'm not the best-qualified person to say what draws people here or what makes people come here because I was already here. But definitely the city is one of the things I like to write about. It's there in *The Intuitionist*. It's there in *Zone One*, and so along with pop culture and race and technology it's one of my subjects that I'm attracted to. The voice of those essays comes out of a chapter in *John Henry Days* where I was trying to have this sort of impressionistic voice—I was writing a chapter about a country fair in a small town—and the voice that's in the *Colossus* essays I first started working on in *John Henry Days*, and I really liked the voice. I liked switching perspectives. The impressionistic sentences, zooming in for a tight shot and pulling back for a larger view. So I wanted to use that voice to write essays about rush hour or Times Square or the Brooklyn Bridge. And it was a side project; it wasn't a novel. I didn't know what it would add up to. I wrote one essay and then put it down for six months, then wrote another. After 9/11 I wrote the essay that is the introduction to *Colossus*, and it seemed like the book I was working on was a bit irrelevant compared to writing about New York and what happened in my hometown. So instead of having *Colossus* on the back burner I started working on it full-time, and I felt better about things once the book was done.

The Rumpus: All of your books are so different—from style to content to structure. I always approach each of your books knowing that it will be very different than the last one. What is the process like when you're starting a new book?

Whitehead: I always have a few ideas that are percolating, and then after I've finished a book and it's a year later and things are sort of festering and things are disgusting in my house and I have to get back to work, whatever project I keep thinking about is the one I end up working on. Sort of a very simple process of elimination. If I have three ideas and I'm working on one more than the others that sort of tells me that I should work on that one. In terms of why everything is different, each book is different than the one before because I'm so bored of what I just finished I want to work on something different. The next book becomes an antidote to what I did before. So *Sag Harbor* is very cheerful, a lot of jokes—it deals with a certain kind of optimistic part of my personality. So that's one part of my personality. Then *Zone One* becomes how I register some of the darker aspects of my personality. The structure of *The Intuitionist*, which is very plot-heavy, finds its antidote in *John Henry Days*, which has a very loose structure, a lot of different voices, and doesn't have a very controlled structure. Basically, I'm definitely done with what I did last time, and so I want to avoid repeating myself.

The Rumpus: Do you ever think about what kind of writer you want to be? Or what you want to accomplish with your career?

Whitehead: I try to challenge myself. With *Zone One*, which borrows from horror movies, it's a challenge to figure out this form—what I want to keep and what I want to throw away—so I want to keep growing as a writer. I find myself doing unexpected projects and sort of challenging my idea of where I am in my career or what I'm supposed to be doing. In fact, I'm not supposed to be doing anything, just finding projects that are challenging to me. I want to be a writer who keeps growing and figuring out new things, and hope-fully people will follow me along as I publish these things.

The Rumpus: You have written about your interest in horror movies, espe-cially your love of George Romero and *Night of the Living Dead.* Why do you think zombies are so compelling to us?

Whitehead: I don't know why other people find them interesting, but for me they are a way of talking about how I feel about people. So zombies are a rhetorical prop for me. Elevators are a rhetorical prop for me in *The Intuitionist.* They allow me a certain way of talking about how I feel about myself and other people and strangers and people I love. So the various different ways that Mark Spitz encounters the living dead in *Zone One* pro-vides different ways of looking at what it is to walk around the world. The way I wrestle with monsters is what made me write *Zone One.*

The Rumpus: Would you ever want to write a movie?

Whitehead: Yeah, I like movies. I've written screenplays as a sort of pro-crastination thing for me. I'll work for a couple months on this idea that's been kicking around, and then, like thirty pages in, I'll just go try a novel because it's a lot easier. That's what I know. So why am I killing myself?

The Rumpus: Did you always want to be a writer?

Whitehead: As a kid I was reading comic books and Stephen King, and it seemed like writing stories about werewolves and superheroes would be a pretty good gig. So, yeah, I watched a lot of movies, read a lot of comic books. Writing movies or writing comic books—like writing *Spider-Man—* would be a really great job. I thought that at a really early age.

The Rumpus: You write a lot about technology in both novels and essays. How do you think technology will affect literature?

Whitehead: I think being a writer was a crappy job when you just had typewriters. It was crappy when we just had ink and paper. And it's sort of crappy now. It's always just you and the page. That doesn't change. In terms of the economics, yes, obviously, the rise of ebooks and how people choose to read books has a big effect on the economics of the game. But whether people are buying them on paper or downloading them, there's still some poor wretch in a room who is trying to write a poem, write a story, write a novel. And so my job doesn't change. It's just how people receive it and eco-nomic conditions on the ground change, but that doesn't affect what I write.

The Rumpus: Do you feel you have to compete with more things now? That there are more distractions for people?

Whitehead: I write books and either people read them or they don't read them. The rise of Facebook or ebooks doesn't change the difficulty level of writing sentences and thinking up new ideas.

The Rumpus: How do you think about writing essays versus writing fiction? These two different mediums—are there commonalities, or do they feel very different to you?

Whitehead: I became a writer working at the *Village Voice,* and that sort of taught me how to sit down for five hours and not get distracted and hand things in on time and be my own boss. So I started off as a critic, which is technically nonfiction. I call myself a novelist, but the essays that come out—I do one or two a year—they are sort of more fun. I don't get assigned that often, but I like the idea of finishing something in a couple days as opposed to years. So a lot of the time when I write an essay, I have an idea, and I can execute it in a couple of days and then move on. So that's really nice. I work on these in-between my novels. That said, I'm working on an expansion of a poker article I wrote last year, so I'm working on a small nonfiction book about poker. Writing nonfiction is different than writing fiction—the poker book is first-person voice, a lot of jokes. I'm sort of worried about what magazine it's for, what the readership is for the magazine, whether you're working with someone else, so there are different ways of writing. And writing a comic novel is different from writing a very linear novel or a loosely structured novel, so there are just different ways of getting at the world. There are just different ways of talking about how it is to walk around on earth.

The Rumpus: Do you feel like you have any obligation to make the world a better place with your books? Or change people? Or is it just about telling a good story?

Whitehead: I don't think there is an obligation, nor is it about story. I write the books that I'm compelled to, and I definitely learn things about the world when I write them. I hope that other people get something out of them, enjoy them, see the world differently when they're done. I can't say that you should extract this or that value from my books explicitly. They are up for interpretation. In terms of the obligation, I think we're all individuals on this planet, trying to scratch our way through the day, and if you're writing a book exposing atrocities in Rwanda or writing a murder mystery set in a mountain village, I think both ways of spending your time are valid. And both books are probably fine to read.

The Rumpus: What's the best book you've read lately?
Whitehead: *Heat* by Bill Buford. I got around to reading that this spring, and that was really good. I just finished *Gone Girl* by Gillian Flynn, and that was a nice way to spend a couple days. I would highly recommend those two.

Colson Whitehead: Each Book an Antidote

Nikesh Shukla / 2013

This interview was originally published in *Guernica*, April 24, 2013. Reprinted with permission of *Guernica* magazine.

Without Colson Whitehead, I would have left the song "Roxanne, Roxanne" by UTFO consigned to the bins of electro and early hip hop I abandoned years ago. Luckily, it was rescued in the pages of *Sag Harbor*.

Without Colson Whitehead, and *Sag Harbor*, I wouldn't have written my first novel. There was something about its episodic structure, its well-timed comedy; instead of relying on aggressive signposting of jokes or employ "ker-azee" similes to get the laugh (as many "funny" books do), Whitehead simply offers quotable dialogue and brilliantly observed characters.

Colson Whitehead is funny. And he's one of those brave writers that writers aspire to emulate because he never rests in any comfort zone: He flips genres, from noir to bildungsroman to zombie horror to history, while maintaining a steady voice, with those delectable turns of phrase, often mistakenly described as wry. It's more than that: it's knowing; it's full of energy.

That's Colson Whitehead for me. From *The Intuitionist*'s surreal study of spirituality and race, against the backdrop of elevator inspector cults, to his depiction of the horror and banality of living in a postapocalyptic dystopia in his latest novel, *Zone One*, and that Twitter account, lighting up with surreal pop culture jokes, well . . . that's why this guy brings out the sycophant in me. He is a writer I envy.

I recently interviewed Colson as part of the *Subaltern* podcast, speaking with him over Skype about zombies, genres, race, and New York.

Guernica: You're often referred to as an African American author. People still refer to me as a British Asian writer, and I've always thought that it's something I could shake off after a couple more novels. Do you wear the label of African American author proudly?

Whitehead: Twenty years ago, when I started writing, I didn't define myself as an African American writer. Then you write books and you're focused on what's inside your books, and that kind of term is generally used on the outside, by the critical establishment. These days I find myself wanting to avoid being pigeonholed, ghettoized, held in a different category [than] other authors. And when people ask me if I'm a black writer or just a writer who happens to be black, I tend to say that it's either a dumb question or a question which happens to be dumb. I'm an African American writer. I'm a lazy writer. I'm a writer who likes to watch *The Wire*. I'm a writer who likes to eat a lot of steak.

Guernica: Are there any ways in which the label is at all useful?

Whitehead: When I was a kid, I'd go to the African American section in the bookstore, and I'd try and find African American people I hadn't read before. So in that sense the category was useful to me, but it's not useful to me as I write. I don't sit down to write an African American zombie story or an African American story about elevators. I'm writing a story about elevators which happens to talk about race in different ways, or I'm writing a zombie novel, which doesn't have that much to do with being black in America. That novel is really about survival.

Guernica: It's not mentioned until quite late in *Zone One* that the character is black. It's not something that drives the story.

Whitehead: Yeah, on one level it's not that important. The apocalypse is what I was thinking of. I'm not sure how the debate plays out in your country, England, but over here, once Obama was elected, there was a certain sense in which people said, "Oh, so no one's racist anymore." As if some magical spell had been cast, and suddenly no one was racist here anymore. Obviously, that isn't true.

Guernica: I feel now that the eighties are back in fashion in the UK; it's almost like racism's back in fashion too. The other day I was called a "Paki" to my face, and my first reaction was that it sounded weird because I hadn't been called that since childhood. I think we might be behind America at the moment.

Whitehead: I think the discussion here is very superficial. The recent American election campaigns showed this. There was race-baiting, and racially coded language used by some Republican candidates. There are underlying narratives which are still pretty potent. I think you're only postracial when you stop asking if you're postracial. When the Neanderthals finally stopped asking themselves if they were in a post–saber tooth society, that's when they were post–saber tooth.

Guernica: Although maybe that's metapostracial because they're still talking about the thing that they no longer are anymore . . .
Whitehead: [*laughs*] That's true. We don't go around saying, "Oh, I haven't seen a saber-tooth for a while." I think it's when we finally stop asking the question of whether we are or not in this place or that place—that's when we're finally done with it.

Guernica: Your books often have an allegorical element but also span genres. I think you've probably done the noir allegory, the historical, the coming-of-age allegory, horror allegory . . . How do you decide where to go next, and how do you decide what to commit to with your projects?
Whitehead: When you put it like that it sounds a bit perverse. I think I just don't want to do the same thing over and over again, so on one level each book becomes an antidote to the one [that] came before. So *The Intuitionist* is very compact and linear, with a very strong plot, and the character is very repressed. I was really sick of that book when I was done with it. *John Henry Days* has a lot of different voices, a much bigger cast, has a lot more humor. And that allows me to just challenge myself: Can I do a book that has less plot? Can I learn the rules of a horror novel, and adapt it to my own concerns about the world? Can I do a coming-of-age novel that doesn't remind me of all the stuff I hate about coming-of-age novels? So I'm trying to keep it fresh for me. I'm just trying to not bore myself. If I can do a detective novel and if I can do a horror novel, then why do it again? To keep the work challenging I have to keep moving.

Guernica: And what's next?
Whitehead: I'm not really sure. I've been trying to take more of a break than I usually take. I've been making notes for something and just trying to rest and read some books and hang out with my kid. Trying to get off the treadmill for a while.

Guernica: Do you view your work as allegorical, in a sense that it's commenting, at one level, on the concerns of the time in which it was written?

Whitehead: *The Intuitionist* and *Apex Hides the Hurt* definitely have their allegorical gestures. And I've never really thought about *Zone One* in that way, but I think just having characters moving across a wasteland will always seem allegorical to some. That sort of aspect is more or less present depending on what I'm trying to do in each book. I like the way that elevators in *The Intuitionist* allowed me to do a kind of cultural critique. I think the critique of social systems plays out differently in *Sag Harbor*. And I think each book has its own way of accommodating my concerns, whether it's about race, America, technology, the city. *Zone One* allowed me to talk about the city in a certain type of way [that was different from], for example, *The Intuitionist*.

Guernica: Did *Zone One* cause any backlash among zombie nerds?
Whitehead: It's funny. When I started that book I felt I came from a very sincere place of zombie love. I'm from the first generation that had the VCR, so in junior high before I started going out I spent my weekends renting horror movies. Watching those was a way my family bonded. So first and foremost I wanted to salute Romero's work and postapocalyptic movies I'd seen as a kid. I felt like people who liked that kind of stuff would embrace it, and that the so-called literary establishment, whatever that is, would be a bit more reluctant, or snobbish. And actually I think people who read my previous books embraced *Zone One* even if they'd never seen a horror movie or read a horror novel. And the gore hounds who are like "How come he's just wandering around thinking the whole time?" obviously want more action. But I kept all my trademark boring parts in the book.

Guernica: With a few zombie films like *28 Days Later*, I understand certain zombie fans got upset that the zombies in the movie were able to run . . .
Whitehead: I guess I think the world's big enough for all kinds of zombies. You can have yours, and I can have mine. I think by going with slow zombies in *Zone One* I maybe have been asserting my own kind of zombie snobbery, but I don't begrudge the youngsters their tackling, running, jumping zombies.

Guernica: Your books often make your readers laugh. What is it that makes you laugh?
Whitehead: I guess just people being people. Stepping back and observing the absurdity of our daily interactions. I talked about watching horror movies as a kid, but I also grew up watching the movies of George Carlin

and Richard Pryor at an early age. So I think in my fiction there's a kind of cultural critique of what they're doing. If I can accommodate my sense of humor in my books I'm glad. *John Henry Days*, which has a lot of different kinds of jokes in it, was a nice relief to write. *Sag Harbor* is funny, I hope. As I get older and write more books I'm definitely allowing the humorous side of my personality more rein in my work.

Guernica: One of the reasons *Sag Harbor* interests me is that lots of writers write a coming-of-age story as their first book. But you had a body of work established and then wrote *Sag Harbor*, which is quite a straight coming-of-age tale, and it seemed to get more attention than the previous novels.
Whitehead: That novel is my take on a traditionally realist genre, the coming-of-age novel. I was wearing realist drag in the same way that I have worn detective drag or horror drag in my other books. I think by avoiding certain expectations of plot and a certain kind of narrative satisfaction I'm doing my own kind of version of it.

Guernica: There's a sense in which each chapter of *Sag Harbor* contains its own discrete story, is its own episode.
Whitehead: Yeah. I don't think the chapters can stand alone, they work best in concert, but I did want each chapter to have its own self-contained topic that it was concerned with, as if they were mini-essays on summer or being a kid or finding your voice. I wanted to be true to the rhythms of summer by not packing the book with too much action. My character Benji is a bit smarter on Labor Day than he was at the beginning of the summer, and that's the most that the majority of us can hope for as we go through life. I slowed down the action and thought about what happens in each day.

Guernica: The book also came across as an ode to hip hop. Do you still listen to that kind of music?
Whitehead: Not so much with new hip hop. That book took me back to eighties music, and I've kind of been stuck in a nostalgic eighties hip-hop, postpunk groove ever since I wrote it. I'm not really up on what's new. I'm still listening to Run-DMC twenty-five years later. In the same way that the baby boomers in America were forcing sixties music and Motown down our throats, now people of my generation are forcing Tears for Fears and old hip hop upon others.

Guernica: New York is such a prevalent backdrop to your work. What do you love about the city? Are there things you love that visitors now won't discover?

Whitehead: Well, I guess just what it was like to live here in the seventies. It was so dirty, you were constantly on guard from predators, and it's so cleaned up now that thinking about how it used to be with the danger and the garbage and buildings on fire. I didn't have to do that much research to present a postapocalyptic New York in *Zone One* because I basically grew up in that New York. That old New York is gone, and that's one thing that's undiscoverable now but I explore in my fiction. Another thing I love about New York is getting lost but not worrying, just wandering and wandering, knowing that there's always a subway only ten blocks away in any direction. There's always a new neighborhood to discover, a new place to lose your bearings in, and yet however alien it seems you can escape. You can always get a cab. All of life's problems can be solved by hailing a cab.

The Confession Book:
Colson Whitehead

Noah Charney / 2016

From *Versopolis.com*. First published in the *European Review of Poetry, Books, and Culture* (2016). Reprinted with permission of Noah Charney.

Noah Charney: Tell me a scent, sound, or taste that you associate with your childhood.

Colson Whitehead: Okay, well, I guess it would be my dad's grilled pork chops. He was obsessed with grilling. They weren't always as moist as you'd like, but sometime around seventh grade he started doing these thin-cut pork chops with barbecue sauce. They remind me of the freedom of summer, my father finally finding a hobby. It helped me become the amateur griller/smoker that I am today.

NC: Ah-ha! Do you have any Colson Special recipes?

CW: Sure. My lemongrass wings with Thai bird chili, fish sauce, ginger, cilantro.

NC: Oh man, you're not messing around.

CW: Oh yes. I may like them more than anyone else, but I make them once a month or so.

NC: Tell me about the first time you played poker and thought to yourself, Hey, I really like this.

CW: In college I drifted between Hearts and Bridge. Senior year of college, after dinner my roommates and I would play Bridge for about four hours and drink a case of beer. We did that all fall and spring semester. In terms of finding a real connection with poker, it was in my early twenties. My friends and I started a weekly Sunday game. Five or six people. A great way to keep in touch with everybody. The host usually cooked. That's where I was introduced to Hold 'em. It took me a few years, though, before I realized I didn't actually know how to play Hold 'em properly.

NC: Do you ever watch televised poker matches? I'm wondering if those are interesting for people who really know poker, like you do.

CW: I've cut back since finishing the book. It'll probably take me awhile to get back into watching poker for fun, as opposed to work. The great innovation, about twelve years ago, was when they started to show the down cards, with a camera that would allow viewers and the commentator to see how the person was playing because you could see their down cards. That contributed to the explosion of televised poker and the popularity of the World Series. Before that it was quite boring to watch, but this allowed for a more packaged experience.

NC: There are some games that seem like good conduits for allegory and exploring the human condition. In your hands, poker is certainly one of them. Chess is an obvious example. Bridge. Whereas Checkers, for instance, doesn't seem to work. What is it about certain games that make them good vehicles for exploring ideas and people, while other games don't function at the same level?

CW: I think the money helps! If you keep losing money in poker, you want to get better; you start understanding the deeper physics of the game. It's a good lure. I've always been interested in board games. I'm very fond of Monopoly. I'm a pretty mellow guy, but for some reason Monopoly tends to bring out my character flaws. No one will play with me anymore because I turn into a different person! In terms of the metaphor of Monopoly . . . The capitalist drive to build, wipe out your enemies, make the most money. It's probably the only place where I allow myself to be a proper American capitalist.

NC: Which figurine do you use?

CW: Always the shoe. I like to come from humble origins only to have my group of reds and greens take over the board.

NC: Describe your morning routine on a day you'd be writing.

CW: Sometimes I've had that one hour to work a day. When you're busy, if you have kids. My preferred way is a full day open, until 3 or 4 when I pick up the kids. If I have a doctor's appointment at 1, say, then my day may be over before it's started. But ideally I'll get to the computer at 9, 9:30. Do emails, read the papers. 10:30–2:30 is my most productive time; then I start to flag and need lunch. Coffee can take me to 2:30, but then I need some food. If I'm free in the afternoon I'll do another stint of revising, an hour or so, and knock off 'til the next day. In the past I've had a second shift, say 8–10 or 11 at night if I wasn't going out. But I'm too old and tired for that.

NC: Do you have a preferred daily word count you aim for?
CW: Not a daily one but for each week. I think that if a novel's a marathon, eight pages is a good productive week. If I can do seven to nine pages a week, that seems like a good accumulation.

NC: What do you snack on while writing?
CW: Stella d'Oro breadsticks, Triscuits, and barbecue potato chips.

NC: I've now done over a hundred of these "How I Write" interviews, and so I occasionally like to ask several authors the same question if their work runs parallel. I asked this of Ben Percy and Peter Straub, and I thought I'd ask you, too. What do you think it is about certain archetypal monsters, like zombies, that allow us to see in them an allegory for the human condition? And why are some monsters too specific or generic to function in this way?
CW: Well, take the *Creature from the Black Lagoon*. It was a big hit when it came out, but it hasn't had staying power in the popular consciousness. It's just a scary monster from the darkness, without anything larger behind it. In terms of zombies, they are a recent archetype, over the last forty years. I can't say why it appeals to other people, but for me the act of transformation of a loved one, a friend or family member or neighbor, into the monster they've always hidden . . . I guess that's the transformation into the monster they've always been but kept hidden from you is very profound for me. My zombies are the Romero zombies, people in *Invasion of the Body Snatchers*. They look like humans, but then a switch goes off and they stop being humans. That animates *Zone One* and is based on my early exposure to *Night of the Living Dead, Dawn of the Dead*.

NC: What has to happen on page one, and in chapter one, to make for a successful book that urges you to read on?
CW: It's always the first page. Some startling arrangement of words, a new perspective, a kind of authority that says, "You're going to keep going," or "You have no idea where this is going," or "This book is exactly for you."

NC: What was the last book you read where you thought, Yeah, this book is exactly for me?

CW: Just recently *Authority* by Jeff VanderMeer. It just came out this spring. A mixture of Tarkovsky's *Stalker* and Lovecraft. A really cool fusion of the two kinds of stories I like. The authority that VanderMeer establishes on the first page is astonishing.

NC: What is guaranteed to make you laugh?
CW: I gravitate towards absurd humor. I can't think of an example, but an image or a joke that captures what is both funny and tragic about the human existence.

NC: What is guaranteed to make you cry?
CW: Now that I have two children, anything involving danger to kids. Something that activates an emotional reaction that I'd rather suppress for most of my days, but it's kicked into gear by an image or something.

NC: This is perhaps a funny question for a writer who has touched on zombies, but if you could bring back to life one deceased person, who would it be and why?
CW: Huh. I'm gonna go with Steve Jobs. The Apple line has gotten a little predictable in the last few years, and I need some new toys.

NC: What advice would you give to an aspiring author?
CW: It's a hard job, a terrible job, and it doesn't get any easier. All you can do is find whatever sort of delusion works for you to keep going.

NC: What would you like carved onto your tombstone?
CW: There's a private detective agency next to my old apartment in Brooklyn. We had to call them one time because of some neighborhood issues. The slogan for this detective agency was "At Best, We Tried."

NC: That's underwhelming.
CW: Maybe it wasn't totally thought out, but their heart was in the right place. So "At Best, He Tried."

NC: I wonder who their PR agent was who came up with that one. And one last question, Colson. Tell us something about yourself that is largely unknown and perhaps surprising.
CW: I really love Jolly Ranchers. Cherry. Sour Apple. But they keep cracking my teeth. I'm a big cruncher, and it's taken its toll . . .

Colson Whitehead: Oprah, American History, and the Power of a Female Protagonist

Stephenie Harrison / 2016

From *BookPage*, August 12, 2016. Reprinted with permission from Bookpage.com. Copyright ©2016 BookPage.

Colson Whitehead's sixth novel may be his best yet. An ambitious, imaginative tour de force, *The Underground Railroad* is the story of Cora, a slave who escapes from a plantation in Georgia via an actual underground railroad. The novel has achieved almost universal praise since it was released and became an Oprah Book Club selection. We gave Whitehead a call to talk about Oprah, historical research, Donald Trump, and writing truth vs. fact.

Stephenie Harrison: First and foremost, congratulations on the buzz that *The Underground Railroad* has been receiving! When I checked the Amazon bestseller list earlier today, the only book that is outranking you in Literature & Fiction is the new Harry Potter book, so that must be kind of exciting for you.
Colson Whitehead: Yeah, definitely. There's no hope of ever beating Harry Potter, but I think the book is doing pretty well. It's definitely been a crazy week—very happy and gleeful—with everything that's happened.

SH: Obviously the other big news is that Oprah just announced that she has selected *The Underground Railroad* for her book club, her first selection in nearly a year and a half. Can you tell me a little bit about how you reacted when you found out that the book had been picked?
CW: It was something that was pretty wild because I had handed in the book four months before, so I wasn't even thinking about reviews or what

would happen to [the book]. But I was doing a reading at Duke University, and I was checking my email on the plane right as it was landing. There was a voicemail from my agent, and she just said one word, "Oprah."

I immediately started cursing. I was trying not to curse because I was on a plane and people were looking at me, but I couldn't hold it in. And then that started this whole crazy ride where I couldn't tell anybody [that she had picked it], and I had to lie to people's faces . . . when she mentioned [*The Underground Railroad*] in her magazine in June, and people said to me "Wouldn't it be great if she picked it?" I was like, "Huh, yeah. But that will never happen, though." So I'm really glad that the news is finally out there.

SH: Is it weird knowing that now when people Google your name that Oprah's name comes up in conjunction?
CW: Well, I was a teenager when she first came into the cultural landscape, so she's always been this huge cultural figure to me. Her book club started around the time that I started publishing. But when you're writing about elevator inspectors, you don't necessarily think you're going to have a lot of mass appeal. I've always loved giving my weird takes on the world and writing books that sound a little oddball and maybe even turn some people off, so with Oprah giving her endorsement, that really cuts through the odd description on the book cover and will hopefully help the book make its way to more readers.

SH: In an article about the craft of writing, you wrote, "Don't go searching for a subject; let your subject find you. You can't rush inspiration." With that in mind, can you share how this book found you?
CW: Just to clarify, that was for a parody article about writing advice, but like any writing cliché, there is a bit of truth in it.

I had the idea for the book about sixteen years ago, recalling how when I was a kid, I thought the Underground Railroad was a literal railroad, and when I found out it wasn't, I was disappointed. So I thought it was a cool idea, and then I thought, Well, what if it actually was a real railroad? That seems like a cool premise for a book. But I had just finished up a research-heavy project and wasn't up for that kind of ordeal again, and I didn't feel mature enough or up to the task. But every couple of years, when I was between books, I would pull out my notes and ask myself if I was ready, and inevitably I would realize that I wasn't really up for it. It wasn't until about two years ago that I really committed to the idea. I had the idea for a novel, but the narrator was very similar to the narrator in my previous book, *The Noble Hustle*, a sort of wise-cracking depressive. And rather than repeat myself, I decided to challenge myself and do the book I found scary to do. When I floated the idea out to people, they seemed really excited about it in a way that was new, so I thought that seemed like it was an idea worth pursuing.

SH: Given that *The Noble Hustle* was about your real-life experiences competing in the 2011 World Series of Poker, would you say that it had you in the mindset to take a gamble?

CW: I guess you could say that! But really, every book is a gamble. Can I pull it off? Will the idea defeat me? Am I up to the task? There's always that kind of fear about what you're about to take on. Figuring out how to overcome it and sidestep the danger and fear is important.

SH: After sitting with this idea for sixteen years, is there anything you can point to as the catalyst that made you feel like you were ready to tell this story?

CW: Honestly, so much time had passed that I finally asked myself, "Why am I putting this off? Why am I afraid to do this?" Slavery is a daunting concept to contemplate, and it's daunting to put your characters through the kind of brutality that telling a truthful story about the topic requires. So those things definitely gave me pause. But I'm older now and I have kids, and both of those things pulled me out of my twenty-something selfishness and gave me a new perspective on my characters and the world. I think that becoming a better writer, becoming a more-well-rounded person and wanting to present a real challenge to myself all played a part as well.

SH: Do you feel that becoming a parent has played an important role in your evolution as a writer?

CW: There is a different kind of empathy that I have for my characters now. I used to joke that after my daughter was born that instead of shooting someone, now it would maybe just be a flesh wound. It's a lot harder to kill characters off, though I have gotten over that. You come to empathy in different ways and writing this book now as opposed to sixteen years ago made a big difference in how the characters turned out.

SH: *The Underground Railroad* is rooted in historical fact and captures the brutal and painful realities of what it was to be black in America during the time of slavery. What kind of research did you do when writing this book?

CW: Primarily I read slave narratives. There are a few histories of the Underground Railroad; one of the first ones I read, which proved the most useful was *Bound for Canaan* by Fergus Bordewich. That gave me an overview of the railroad, but the main thing was just reading the words of former slaves themselves. There are the big famous slave narratives by Frederick Douglass and Harriet Jacobs, but in order to get people back to work, the government in the 1930s hired writers to interview former slaves. We're talking eighty-year-old and ninety-year-old people who had been in bondage when they were kids and teenagers, and that provided a real variety of slave experiences for me to draw upon. It gave me a real taste for the expansiveness and breadth of plantation life as well as the slang and small details that help make the world rich.

SH: Even though this is a work of historical fiction, I don't think there will be a single reader who makes it through *The Underground Railroad* without drawing parallels between Cora's world and our modern reality. As a writer, how much did you lean into and draw energy from the present-day and current events when writing this book?

CW: Well, the country is still pretty racist, so it doesn't take that much of a leap to draw parallels between black life a hundred and fifty years ago and now. For example, the parallel between the slave patrollers two hundred years ago who had the power to stop any black person—free or slave—and demand to see their papers and "stop and frisk" policies now. You don't have to work hard to see the continuum of oppression in this country.

SH: How does it feel having this book published in the same year that we could conceivably see Donald Trump elected as the next president of the United States?

CW: It's scary to contemplate a Trump presidency, whether you're black or white! Seeing some of the rhetoric at his rallies, it reminds me of when I was writing the book in 2015 and wondering if I was going too far in some of the lynching scenes or being a bit too extreme. But the answer is no: the lynch-mob mentality is still around, as is the demonization of the other whether it's the African, the newly-arrived Irish immigrant, or now the Muslim immigrant. Fear and prejudice is a constant in American life. It's gotten better by degrees, of course, but the world of Cora is not that far removed from our own.

SH: You chose Cora, a female protagonist, as the book's core, and you largely explored the parameters of the slave's world from the perspective of women. Why did you decide to do this?

CW: I guess I like to change it up from book to book, and I had had a certain kind of meditative "dude narrator" for my last three books. So it just seemed time to mix it up. The narrator of my first book was a woman, and I like that people think that my female protagonists work, though I also think that if you have a plumber come to your house, you wouldn't commend them for getting your drain clean. I think as a writer, it's your job to present realistic protagonists and a supporting cast.

SH: But you have mentioned that when you initially conceived of the book, you had a male at the center, so was there a moment when you felt that the story worked better with a woman protagonist?

CW: Over the sixteen years, the protagonist migrated: I've had it as a man, a man looking for a child, a man looking for his wife. When I finally committed to the book, I hadn't explored a mother-daughter relationship before, and it seemed time to take that on.

Also, the black female experience in slavery was so terrible and different from the male experience that it seemed important to illuminate some of the specific history of African women in slavery.

SH: What was it about the character of Cora that you found the most compelling as a writer?

CW: When you drop a character into the midst of slavery, they're going to endure a lot of brutality and hardship. I was certainly rooting for Cora as she goes farther and farther north, and I admire her gradual awareness of the world and that she gets wiser and wiser with every step. There are certainly a lot of reversals of fortune that occur, but she keeps fighting. And that's very admirable.

SH: When we look at the American literary canon, there are already some incredibly powerful and moving classics about slavery and the pre–Civil War black experience like *Beloved, Kindred, Uncle Tom's Cabin,* and *The Known World.* What do you think *The Underground Railroad* brings to the table when it comes to contributing something new to the black slave narrative?

CW: It's not really for me to say what it brings that's new; that's really something that other people can say, or not say. For me, I just try to bring my own perspective to whatever I'm writing about, whether it's a coming-of-age novel or a nonfiction book of immersive journalism. You can't worry about what people have done before, you just have to trust that you have something new to say and execute your vision as well as possible.

SH: When you think about the book, do you think about it uniquely as a slave narrative or, in your mind, it's about more than the black slave experience?

CW: To me, it's a novel about slavery, Americanness, and perseverance.

SH: This is your first explicitly historical novel. Did working within a fixed historical context challenge you in ways that your previous novels didn't?

CW: It's always a challenge to figure out different forms. Since I do change genres and forms a lot, that's always a big part of the task early on.

The first chapter in Georgia I tried to make realistic and stick to the historical record, and then after that, I wanted to stick to the truth of the black experience but not necessarily the facts. As we go to South Carolina and Indiana and the different states that Cora goes to, I am playing with history and time, moving things up to talk about the Holocaust, the Tuskegee Syphilis Experiment, and the eugenics movement. So in some sense, it's not really a historical novel at all because I'm moving things around. Once she gets out of Georgia and starts on her journey, I didn't feel that I had to stick to the historical record, and that gave me much more latitude to play in terms of the themes and different concepts to work with.

SH: Although you have an incredibly eclectic back catalog that includes a zombie apocalypse novel and a book about coming of age in the Hamptons, one overarching theme in your novels is the issue of race and the black experience in America. In your own words, how does *The Underground Railroad* fit into and expand upon your oeuvre to date?

CW: I think it fits in with some of my books because it deals with race and American history, which are two things that I'm interested in, along with technology and pop culture. With some of my books, like *John Henry Days*, I can get a lot of my preoccupations in there, and then sometimes I'm finding different ways of talking about some of my favorite subjects. While I've written about race in most of my books, if you're actually going to the original sin of slavery, it requires a different tactic. I think the ironic voice of *Sag Harbor* that Benji has provides one way of talking about race, and then a clear-eyed view about the true brutality of slavery requires a different kind of voice and tactic.

SH: As a follow-up to that last question, although you've made a name for yourself by picking wildly disparate subjects and adopting very different styles with each novel is there a topic or genre that you'll never touch as a writer?

CW: Never say never, but I'm probably not going to write a book about football or yoga . . . but you never know!

SH: Do you believe that there are benefits to tackling difficult topics like slavery and race through the medium of fiction (and perhaps film) as opposed to newspaper articles and nonfiction pieces?
CW: Each form is different and has its advantages and disadvantages. As a novelist, I get to make up stuff. When you're a historian or a nonfiction writer, you have to stick to the facts, but making up things is the fun part for me.

SH: *The Underground Railroad* clearly pays homage to Jonathan Swift's *Gulliver's Travels*, with Cora's journey to each new state analogous to Gulliver's voyage to strange new lands. Do the similarities end there, or, like Swift's novel, do you also view your novel as a satire?
CW: It's not a satire. Once I thought about making each state its own place with its own set of rules, the first analogy for me was *Gulliver's Travels*. I'm not a *Gulliver's Travels* fanatic, but . . . I think it's a good structure: It's episodic—much like *The Odyssey* and *Pilgrim's Progress*, where a person is on a journey and they're being tested along the way with different episodes that have different allegorical freight. The structure itself has been around for a while. Early on it seemed like a good way of framing it, and it became my default way of describing the book.

SH: Lately there has been a lot of discussion about white privilege in America and systemic racism that is propagated by whitewashed media and entertainment. As a black writer, why do you believe it is so important for readers to actively diversify their reading?
CW: I'm not going to tell people what to read, and I haven't said that it is important for us to diversify our literature. Publishing as an institution in the world is racist because the world is racist. I do think you are probably a more-well-rounded person if you read books by men and women and people with different-colored skin. But I don't care if you do or not.

SH: For readers who are interested in checking out a more diverse array of authors, can you recommend any that you think are particularly worth their time?
CW: Sure. There are a lot of authors that I like: Toni Morrison, ZZ Packer, Junot Díaz, Adam Johnson, and Kelly Link all come to mind. I'm excited to pick up Elena Ferrante and I also like Gish Jen.

SH: Given the subject matter, what has it been like trying to pick passages of this book to read aloud to an audience as you prepare for your upcoming tour?

CW: I really enjoy readings, and I usually read the funny parts because people enjoy them and I remember writing the jokes. But this book has very few jokes compared to my other work, so I'm trying to find bits that are self-contained. Right now I'm reading the part when the slave masters interrupt the birthday party on the plantation, which covers a bit of ground, and it's the first time I mention the Declaration of Independence, which plays a big role in the book. I also choose between the short biographical sections with Dr. Stevens, Ethel, and Caesar; right now I'm reading the Ethel section because it is so different from Cora's experience.

SH: One of the most vital messages in *The Underground Railroad* is about the power of the written word and the ability to read. What's the most important book you've ever read that you think should be considered required reading?

CW: It's hard to pick one, but in terms of my evolution as a writer, I would say *One Hundred Years of Solitude* by Gabriel García Márquez. I read it when I was in high school, and I read it again before I started this book. As a teenager, it broadened my idea of what a novel could be and as a forty-something it gave me an idea of how a novel could be organized.

SH: Now that you've finished this huge, emotionally draining book, what are your plans and what are you working on next?

CW: I am busy all fall promoting the book, so come January I will take stock. Right now, it's going to be a novel that takes place in Harlem in the 1960s. I've still got a lot to research, so that's all I can say about it!

In Conversation with Colson Whitehead

Boris Kachka / 2016

From *Vulture.com*, August 14, 2016. © 2016 New York Media LLC.
Reprinted with permission of Boris Kachka/Vulture.com.

Colson Whitehead's latest novel, *The Underground Railroad*—rushed last week to early publication after being anointed by Oprah Winfrey—turns the metaphor of the American fugitive–slave network into a literal system of stations traveled by preternatural locomotives. The (painful, beautiful, brilliantly imagined) journey of the slave Cora from a cruel Georgia plantation through a handful of states, each "a state of possibility" portending America's fractured racial history, has gestated in Whitehead's mind for sixteen years—almost as long as he's been roving across his own series of bizarre fictional landscapes. There were the acclaimed early novels, *The Intuitionist* and *John Henry Days*, cheeky and weird extended metaphors for racial and industrial anxiety that earned him a MacArthur genius grant. There was the less admired satire *Apex Hides the Hurt*, followed by the autobiographical *Sag Harbor*, about Whitehead's upbringing as an upper-middle-class black New Yorker. Along came *Zone One*, a joke-splattered zombie thriller, and the midlife-crisis poker stunt memoir *The Noble Hustle*. And then, finally, the unlikely completion of the novel he never thought he'd write, followed by, probably, a level of fame and posterity he'd never imagined. Skinny and dreadlocked in a jaunty short-sleeved plaid shirt, Whitehead sat down with us on Tuesday over a cappuccino near his West Village home.

Boris Kachka: Are you having a good week?
Colson Whitehead: Yeah, the best week of my professional career, so.

BK: You got the call from Oprah months ago and then had to keep it a secret until now. Did you tell your family?

CW: Just my wife, who came out with me to Oprah Land in Southern California, and then we shot the interview that appeared last week. Then for three months people were like, "When's the pub date?" "September." "How do you feel?" "Uh, I feel okay."

BK: Oprah hadn't read your other books, which are very different from this one. Was that weird?

CW: Well, I've been publishing for eighteen years, and I'm sort of used to that because I've switched genres. The readership for *Sag Harbor* was different from people who'd read me before—it was linear and realistic, not as strange as *The Intuitionist*. Did they carry over to *Zone One*, a story about zombies in New York? Some, some not. I'm used to people not caring about my other books.

BK: Did you have any sense, pre-Oprah, that this was going to be your big novel?

CW: I don't go back to a finished book as often as I have with this one, and I'm still very much invested in Cora and Caesar and Mabel. I think going back I can relive those months last fall and feel a sense of accomplishment, and also a weird . . . wonder? I'm still trying to figure out how to put it into words. But I felt like I did a good thing, and I still feel this kind of rush of accomplishment.

BK: How did this concept—of the literal underground railroad—change since you first thought of it years ago?

CW: I had a handwritten page in 2000, and in 2004 I put it on the computer—just a list of "South Carolina, futuristic gene splicing?" Every couple of years I would pull it out and add a sentence and move a couple of things around. Originally, "he" was going to come to New York and then Canada. It was a guy on his own, then a man looking for a child, a child looking for a parent, and finally a daughter looking for a mother. All the states are really just arbitrary.

BK: And you were all set to write a different novel, about a New Yorker having a midlife crisis, when you thought of developing this in 2014. How did you switch gears?

CW: I was on my way to work at Princeton and wrote an email to my editor, Bill Thomas. "Here's another idea." It was a paragraph, and he said, "Sure, whatever you want to do." So I started doing research in the fall. I wrote the first hundred pages in January 2015, and they said, "So do you think you can hand it in for next fall publication?" I still had two hundred pages to go, but I was in a real froth about the book and I said yes. So I finished the thing in early December. Usually it takes me a while to figure out the voice of the narrator, but when I wrote the first chapter, which deals with Cora's grandmother, the voice came fully formed and I stuck with it.

BK: You must have been starting your research just as Michael Brown was shot in Ferguson. Did that, and subsequent shootings, fuel the story in any way?
CW: I think today is the second anniversary of him being killed. But I came of age in New York in the eighties, when Yusuf Hawkins was beaten to death for being in the wrong neighborhood, Michael Stewart was beaten to death by cops for doing graffiti, Eleanor Bumpurs was a mentally unstable woman killed by police. And so I was trained that whenever you leave the house you're a target, even in lovely Manhattan. I think we do get these periodic eruptions, and the conversation changes briefly to police brutality. There hasn't been an uptick in it, just in people recording it. It's not news to me, and I don't know how long our present conversation about the vulnerability of the black body will continue. Since we're not changing the underlying causes, these moments are temporary because our attention has always shifted elsewhere.

BK: Do you think there's been any progress?
CW: Sure—it's very slow progress. We have a black president, and various laws have been implemented. I'm at a big publisher, I'm talking to a big magazine, and I owe my career to writers who have come before me. So things have changed.

BK: There are more writers, too. Chris Jackson edits a lot of them.
CW: How many African American editors are there? But yes, there's [Yaa Gyasi's slavery novel] *Homegoing*, [Brit Bennett's debut] *The Mothers*. You can actually point to young African American writers debuting in their twenties and thirties and all doing different things. But it is incremental; it is slow.

BK: You're well known for comic riffs and wild inventions. *The Underground Railroad* is relatively dialed-back.

CW: I think if I had done it ten years ago, the divisions between the states would have been more stark and more *Gulliver's Travels*–like—each state with its own reality, time period, codes, and customs. And some of that is still in there, but everything's taking place around 1850 in terms of technology and slang. I wanted to be concise. I had given myself free rein to have digressions in various books, and I didn't feel I had to do that anymore. When I got to the section with the Museum of Natural Wonders, I wrote two pages, and I was like, I'm done. I'm not gonna make this a big set piece like I've done in the past and pull out the bombast. It's nice and quiet the way it is now; let's keep it there.

BK: What made you do that? Was it the gravity of the subject?
CW: Well, you can do a lot of jokes in a slavery book. *Flight to Canada* by Ishmael Reed probably has a lot of jokes. But I'd just written a poker book that had a lot of jokes—I tried to cram in as many as I could. I got it out of my system, and then also as I did more research, I wanted to honor all the people who had been in slavery, to the dead, to my ancestors. So even though I play with history and time, in terms of moving the Tuskegee syphilis experiments down and bringing the implications of the Holocaust in, I wanted the first chapter to be as realistic as I could do it. And, yeah, it is a serious subject that didn't seem to warrant my usual satire and joking.

BK: In an essay of tongue-in-cheek advice about choosing a genre, you listed the "Southern Novel of Black Misery." How did you aim to avoid the clichés?
CW: I had my kitsch detector out, so hopefully it was working. I wanted to be realistic to my notion of psychology. We know a lot about PTSD. Well, these are people who experience trauma every day of their lives. How does that manifest itself? How could I make a realistic backdrop for Cora? In my experience, if you get a hundred people in a room, 10 percent are really great, 10 percent are terrible, and the rest are mediocre. But if you go to a plantation where 100 percent have been tortured and abused, they're not on their best behavior. Everyone's out for themselves, fighting for a little piece of land, for an extra bite of food in the morning. In some portrayals of plantation life, there are some sellouts, but most people are sticking together. That just didn't seem true to my understanding of human nature. I was being true to my idea of a traumatized populace under siege, so I didn't worry about kitsch.

BK: Cora's journey seems to encompass almost every feature of black history. One half-black preacher is described as a "beautiful hybrid," and I couldn't help but think of Obama.

CW: Uhm [*laughs*], no, I think there's a tradition of the biracial person who can move through both worlds. But the preacher's antagonist represents respectability politics: We can't save every slave who's damaged; we have to save the ones we can. And we hear that kind of rhetoric today. Pull your pants up; you're too damaged in the inner city to join us in this new America.

BK: That reminds me of someone too.

CW: So, comparing the rhetoric of black progress then and now, it was so similar I didn't have to force it. That was true of comparing slave patrollers to stop-and-frisk now.

BK: You were handcuffed as a teenager in Manhattan—a case of mistaken identity. Have you had other encounters?

CW: Just being stopped. One time my friend was in med school and a cop stopped us. I guess he had MD plates, and the cop said, "I've never seen doctor's plates before."

BK: Is it just a coincidence that you spent almost all of the Obama years not writing about race, except in satirical riffs like "Finally, a Thin President" and "The Year of Living Postracially"?

CW: There were just other things I wanted to talk about. I'm fortunate, being at the same publisher for eight books, that whenever I have an idea, they're like, "Let's do it. We trust you to pull it off." I knew that a zombie book would not particularly appeal to some of my previous readers, but it was artistically compelling, and being able to do a short nonfiction book about poker was really fun and great. But looking back, I was able to say to myself, "Well, you had your book for you. Now I want you to talk about something serious."

BK: You're not done being unserious, are you?

CW: I'm not sure, but in writing this book I was stopping myself from doing things the way I've done in the past—in terms of economy, of a less satirical voice. I gave myself a lot of digressions in *Sag Harbor* and *The Noble Hustle*. And so I don't have to do them anymore. There are ways of tackling material that I felt didn't serve the book and maybe will come back later. But there are clichés about slavery and also clichés I've made myself, ways of writing.

BK: The style of this novel reminds me of Toni Morrison—completely apart from the subject matter. The sentences are more aphoristic, more gemlike, than anything you've ever done.

CW: Yeah, I've been thinking about sentences the last couple of years. My more modern narrators like to have these big clause-heavy sentences, but not in this particular book. I think part of it is that shaping metaphors out of life from the 1850s made some of the similes and analogies simpler. You know, a sentence that comes easily to me is, "The street was busier than a 7-Eleven parking lot on free meth day." I could make a weird modern joke, and that's a long sentence. But when you try to make a simile or a metaphor out of the nouns of 1850s, simplicity and clarity make more sense.

BK: There is a theme in the recent reviews—kind of praising you for putting away childish things. Is that how you see it?

CW: It's an imposed narrative, and it's fine. Eighteen years have passed since my first book, and I do feel older and wiser. And while hopefully I can write a book with humor again, there are certain broad gestures I don't have to do anymore—certain pyrotechnic effects I've gotten out of my system. I felt more in control when I was writing this book. I was teaching a lot, and I was a pretty ruthless editor of my students' fiction. It seemed unfair to spare myself the knife. Putting out all these principles, I should probably apply them to myself! And so I became a much better editor of my own stuff over the last couple of years.

BK: Have you changed in other ways? You've had children.

CW: I guess "mature" is the word. Cora is not someone who would have occurred to me fifteen years ago. I was just younger and more self-centered and didn't have the empathy. Lila Mae in *The Intuitionist* doesn't have a team, but Mark Spitz in *Zone One* and Cora in *The Underground Railroad* have people they can rely on. Not everyone makes it to the other side, but they have a team, a community. I was attracted to the loner in my first couple of books who's apart from all these systems, breaking them down, analyzing them. And Cora is a slave, she's enmeshed in the slave system and has to figure out her way out, and she can't do it alone. She has to rely on other people to give her the notion that she can do it and also show her the path. And, yes, as a parent who's lived longer, you understand what it actually means to have no agency, to see your children, your mother, your relatives, your friends, at the mercy of a capricious master with all that entails. Slavery meant something different to me when I was eight, and twenty, and then now.

BK: But you didn't have to write about slavery, did you?

CW: I would joke about having to do [a slavery novel] at talks, knowing in the back of my head I had this idea sitting there. I started writing in the nineties, so I was free to just have an eccentric career and not conform to some idea of what a black writer has to do. I didn't have the burden of representation. Growing up as a product of the black civil rights movement, I had a lot of different models for black weirdness, whether it's Richard Pryor or James Baldwin or Jimmy Walker.

BK: And you wanted to be weird?

CW: I was very self-conscious starting out. I worked in the book section of the *Village Voice*, and I would see all these new novels come in. I didn't want to write a Gen-X sex-drugs-and-rock-and-roll book, and there was a certain Southern Novel of Black Misery I just couldn't relate to, just being a New Yorker. I didn't want to write something autobiographical. I didn't want to do what I'm supposed to do as a black writer or as a young writer. In *The Intuitionist* I wanted to write about race and a city, and as I started writing about elevators, metaphors of black uplift crept in. It was about race, but in a way that I could handle when I was twenty-seven, just a weird way no one else would do.

BK: *The Underground Railroad* is probably as straight-ahead as you could get. You even reprinted actual classified ads for fugitive slaves. Where did you get them, and why did you open every section with one?

CW: Those are from the University of North Carolina, which digitized their old newspapers. It's fun to make up stuff, but sometimes you can't really compete with the actual rhythms of historical documents. They're only eight lines or so, but they tell so much about the person who's writing them down and the person who fled and the entire culture that enables them to come into being. And writing one for Cora seemed like a nice gift from the narrator to her because I was sort of bummed out about what I was doing to her.

BK: There are some truly horrific scenes in the novel, especially involving slaves who were caught escaping. Were those all real punishments from your research?

CW: You want to set an example, so, yes, you would burn people alive; yes, you would cut off their feet and their hands. I would go back and forth and think, Is that too crazy, and go back to a couple of narratives and think, Actually no. I did originally have a crucifixion, but I couldn't find any evidence of that so I took it out.

BK: You've said you couldn't sit through *12 Years a Slave* after doing that research, but you depicted worse. You must have been a mess.

CW: I was a mess mostly before I started writing. I have a protagonist, and realistically she will be sexually assaulted before the book starts, realistically her mother will be assaulted. So just wrapping my head around what was a realistic backstory for her was terrible. Then I think it has affected how I feel about her at the end of the book. When I reread the last couple of pages, I feel bad for having put her through it.

BK: This is your first book to come out to universal acclaim in a long time. How did you react when *Apex Hides the Hurt* was widely considered a disappointment?

CW: I really liked the voice! I thought it was a really clean narrator, unadorned. But just because you like it, it doesn't mean everyone else will—or will pick up on it. All I could do is just write the next one. Sometimes people will figure out what you're doing, sometimes they won't, but that's out of your hands. And then with *The Underground Railroad*, I assumed I would still have my regular readers, maybe gain a few because it's in the historical mode. Having people like the book this much—and Oprah and the *Times* thing [a stand-alone print excerpt published in the August 7, 2016, edition of the *New York Times*]—it's never gonna happen again. So I should enjoy it, and the next book might be received *Apex*-like.

BK: What is the next book—the midlife-crisis book you were working on?

CW: No, I think I got that out of my system. I don't know if I'll stick to it, but I think it's going to take place in the sixties in Harlem. It's subject to change.

BK: We've talked a lot about how this book is a departure, but what makes it a Colson Whitehead book?

CW: Stepping back, my latest theory is that with the first couple of books, I had some sort of problem I was trying to figure out, or proposition. How do I update this industrial-age anxiety myth for the information age? And then I think *Sag Harbor* and *Zone One* and *Noble Hustle* are about characters finding their way in the world. In *The Underground Railroad* I'm taking both: What if it was an actual railroad, and also, this person had to navigate these different Americas on her way to freedom. The character portrait of the last couple of books merged with the larger abstract question.

BK: Why did you choose to thank bands in your acknowledgments?

CW: With the last eight books, whenever I had two pages to go, I would just put on *Purple Rain* and *Daydream Nation*, and that's been my last-day ritual for the past twenty years. After Bowie died, I said to myself, I want to put this down on paper just so *they know*. And then Prince died after I put the acknowledgments in! Not that he was going read it anyway.

BK: Do you think it was the bleak subject matter that kept you away from this for sixteen years?

CW: Well, I think *Zone One* is pretty bleak, but this one is very grim going. I think I got to a point where I had avoided the book for so many years it was worth examining why I was avoiding it. And it seemed that if it was daunting to tackle slavery, well, maybe the hard thing is the thing you're supposed to be doing.

Colson Whitehead's Subterranean Journey

Hilary Leichter / 2016

From *Electric Literature*, August 18, 2016. Reprinted with permission of Hilary Leichter.

In *The Underground Railroad*, Colson Whitehead's gripping new novel, we are introduced to a metaphor made manifest: an actual railroad, underground. A literal and literary engine for his incredible inquiry into slavery, humanity, and the true nature of America. When Cora is invited to leave, to escape the plantation where she has lived her whole life and take the titular train north, she climbs down the rabbit hole and through different states, both geographical and psychological. She runs through a world fueled by cruelty, ambivalence, and, every so often, kindness. And we see this world with sober eyes by the light of her unsentimental telling.

When discussing this book with a friend (you will want to discuss *The Underground Railroad*, immediately and urgently), our conversation turned to another novel, *Feeding the Ghosts* by Fred D'Aguiar. In that book, the *Zong*, a slave ship headed for America, is overtaken with illness, and the enslaved men and women are thrown overboard. The protagonist, Mintah, manages to somehow lift herself from the water and climb back aboard the ship, perhaps buoyed by ghosts or death. The middle passage is reframed through a fantastic and surreal lens, much in the way Whitehead reframes the metaphor of the railroad. These crossings—one headed towards slavery and one towards freedom—are also somehow crossings-over, passages through time and through the irreal. The journeys take on a particular and uncanny power. At a station stop in Whitehead's novel, Cora stares into the abyss of the terminal, wondering where the railroad ends, where it begins: "As if in the world there were no places to escape to, only places to flee."

Hilary Leichter: There's something irresistible about the central metaphor to your book: an underground railroad that is an actual railroad. Sometimes it feels like descending into Hades, and sometimes it feels like the New York subway system—there's one stop decorated with white tile. The railroad is a kind of character in the book. How did you go about bringing it to life? Where did the metaphor start?

Colson Whitehead: It came from that idea from childhood where you first hear about the Underground Railroad and think it's an actual subway. That was my first association, when I was seven or eight. And then of course I'm not the only person—if you check Twitter for "underground railroad" you'll find high school kids making fun of their friends: "Sam thought the Underground Railroad was an actual railroad!" So this sort of image stays with people. It's majestic. Cora's on the train a couple of times in the book, and I wanted each station to have a different character. Sometimes it's just a hole in the ground; sometimes it's a nicely appointed place to wait, with tables and a candelabra and wine. Sometimes the train is a great locomotive; sometimes it's a boxcar; sometimes it's a handcart. In trying to find a variety of experiences for Cora, I tried to come up with these different subterranean scenarios.

Leichter: When Cora makes her first trip on the railroad, she's given this piece of advice that comes back several times in the book, "Look outside as you speed through, and you'll find the true face of America." After a while, this feels a bit like a joke because the tunnel is completely dark. But is that kind of complete blindness the true face of America? I was also thinking about how when you take a train at night, above ground, and you look outside the window, the face you see reflected is your own.

Whitehead: I think Cora struggles to decode those words of the first station master. Yes, if you look into a tunnel in the ground it's just darkness, and if that's America, what is that saying? When you're on a train, for me, part of the joy is seeing the landscape, the different places you're going through. I'm sure there's probably more than one Amtrak advertisement that says "Take Our Train, See the Country." So I'm having a little bit of fun there with what you can see and what America you're actually seeing outside the window.

Leichter: The book definitely plays with some surreal elements, but they feel completely subsumed by the terrible and violent realities of the plot. I felt that my disbelief was permanently suspended because the horrors of slavery that you depict here continually left me in a similar kind of stunned disbelief. Was it important to you to use this surreal premise to talk about the realities of slavery? Or was it just the particular way that you found into the subject matter?

Whitehead: I wanted to talk about a variety of different things related to Americanness, and the changing concept of race in America. And once I made the choice to have this central fantastic element of a literal underground railroad, it allowed me to play with time and bring in elements of the Holocaust, the Tuskegee syphilis experiments, and things like that. While they're all fantastic elements, I think the voice of the narrator is so matter of fact that they're well integrated into Cora's experience. So when she steps out and sees a skyscraper in 1850s South Carolina, she takes it at face value. When she comes to North Carolina and discovers a place where black people are outlawed and hunted down, it seems like a natural future of the world. So the voice works to integrate some of the absurd but also the truthful elements of her world.

Leichter: Can you tell me a little bit about the process of researching the book? Where did you start?

Whitehead: There are a few histories of the Underground Railroad, not as many as you'd think. The main one I started out with, *Bound for Canaan*, by Fergus Bordewich—it came out a couple of years ago. That was my survey of history of the movement, but my main research was slave narratives. The ones we've heard of that are famous: Frederick Douglass, Harriet Jacobs. But primarily the ones collected by the WPA in the 1930s. To get people back to work, the government gave writers jobs interviewing former slaves who were still alive in 1935. People who were eighty or seventy years old. It provided a real catalog of slave life. Small farms, big plantations. The mechanics of farming and what they ate and the culture of the plantation, all done in this matter-of-fact voice that I ended up using in the book.

Leichter: Was there anything you found that surprised you, or that maybe didn't make it into the final draft of the book?

Whitehead: Things that intrigued me all found their way in, one way or another. I tend to do research to get going, and then if there's something I have to research, I'll do some more research along the way. It breaks up the writing, the monotony of just writing pages every day. So when Dr. Stevens appears in South Carolina, I thought his would be an interesting perspective, fleshing out a supporting character. So I studied grave digging and inanimate research in the early part of the nineteenth century. As the book progressed and different avenues of inquiry presented themselves, I pursued them, weaved them into the book.

Leichter: There are interspersed mininarratives from some of these supporting characters, spread throughout the book. Was that something that you had intended to do, or did it come from being interested in one of those people and wanting to spend a little bit more time figuring them out?

Whitehead: It wasn't so much figuring them out but using them as opportunities to expand the investigation into American history. Ajarry, the first section about Cora's grandmother, was always the prologue. I wanted to have these character portraits in between the chapters, and I would juggle who should go in and who should not go in. Should I focus on Martin or Ethel from North Carolina? Should I have Caesar's voice or Lovey's voice? And you have to obviously be open to changing things, that's the fun of discovery. As I would go along, different characters would provide different ways of talking about the broader themes.

Leichter: Each of your books is so different in scope, in tone, in everything. How important is it to you to immerse yourself in completely new projects and new challenges?

Whitehead: I'm so sick of one thing that the next project has to be pretty different. Whether it's going from a first-person voice that's nimble and jokey, like in *The Noble Hustle,* my book about poker, or going to a third-person expansive voice in *John Henry Days* after *The Intuitionist.* It's a nice way of saying goodbye to the previous book. Before I started this book I had an idea about a writer in New York City, and the voice was very close to the voice of the narrator in *The Noble Hustle,* a version of me. It seemed if I had just done it in *The Noble Hustle,* why do it again? And so I set that book aside and started *The Underground Railroad,* which is very different from my last couple of books.

Leichter: There's a moment early on in the book, where you're describing Cora's fraught relationships with some of the other women on the plantation, and the terrible experiences that they face together. And you write this beautiful sentence: "Sometimes such an experience bound one person to another; just as often the shame of one's powerlessness made all witnesses into enemies." I found this idea profoundly affecting, especially in a contemporary context, where it feels like we witness everything, horrible things, every day, online. Is that something that you were considering?

Whitehead: I don't think I was thinking about our contemporary experience of being in the world, but I was trying to create a plausible psychology for a plantation, using what we know in the early twenty-first century about how people behave, and posttraumatic stress disorder. Of course these slaves aren't "post-" anything, they're in that trauma, living it morning, afternoon, and night. But what is the damaged psychology of the slave? It seems to me, and perhaps this is a dark view of humanity, but if you put people in a room, ten are great, ten are terrible, and in the middle you have the other eighty, who sort of vacillate between being horrible and not-so-horrible. But if you have a hundred people on a plantation who have been brutalized, assaulted, and dehumanized their whole lives, they're not going to be on their best behavior. And so it seemed that a plantation where everyone's helping each other out and is really pleasant to each other didn't fit my idea of humanity. It seemed that it would be every person for themselves.

A Literary Chameleon

Jesse McCarthy / 2016

From *Harvard Magazine* 119.1 (September–October 2016): 32–36, 79. Reprinted with permission of Jesse McCarthy and Harvard Magazine Inc.

Colson Whitehead has written a zombie-apocalypse novel, a coming-of-age novel set in the world of the black elite, a satiric allegory following a nomenclature consultant, a sprawling epic tracing the legend of the African American folk hero John Henry, a suite of lyrical essays in honor of New York City, and an account of drear and self-loathing in Las Vegas while losing $10,000 at the World Poker Series. That work has won him critical acclaim. He received a MacArthur Fellowship in 2002, and has been a finalist for almost every major literary award; he won the Dos Passos Prize in 2012 and a Guggenheim Fellowship in 2013. In an era when commercial pressure reinforces the writerly instinct to cultivate a recognizable voice, his astonishingly varied output, coupled with highly polished, virtuosic prose, makes Whitehead one of the most ambitious and unpredictable authors working today.

He has gained a reputation as a literary chameleon, deftly blurring the lines between literary and genre fiction, and using his uncanny abilities to inhabit and reinvent conventional frames in order to explore the themes of race, technology, history, and popular culture that continually resurface in his work. In a country where reading habits and reading publics are still more segregated than we often care to admit, his books enjoy a rare crossover appeal. His first novel, *The Intuitionist*, is a detective story that regularly turns up in college courses; the zombie thriller *Zone One* drew praise from literary critics and genre fiction fans alike; *Sag Harbor*, about black privileged kids coming of age in the 1980s, was a surprise bestseller.

Beyond the books, Whitehead swims effortlessly in the hyperconnected moment: he maintains an active presence on Twitter, where his sly and dyspeptic observations on the curious and the mundane have gained him a devoted following. A sampling includes sagacious tips for the aspiring writer—"Epigraphs are always better than what follows. Pick crappy epigraphs so you don't look bad"—and riffs on Ezra Pound: "The apparition of these faces in the crowd / Petals on a wet, black bough / Probably hasn't been gentrified though." In the pages of the *New York Times Magazine* and the *New Yorker*, he has wryly dissected contemporary mores and the light-speed metamorphoses of language in the age of social media. In a widely shared essay from last year, he parsed the current attachment to the tautophrase, as in "you do you" and "it is what it is," or Taylor Swift's popularization of "Haters gonna hate." Swift makes an easy target, of course, but Whitehead takes aim at the rhetoric of those in power too, and the narcissism in our culture more generally. He's more gadfly than moralist, but there is a Voltaire-like venom to his sarcasms. "The modern tautophrase empowers the individual," he observes, "regardless of how shallow that individual is."

At forty-six, Whitehead is approaching the midpoint of a successful writing career. He exudes the confidence and ease of a man settled in his craft, and for that reason is also inherently restless, driven to test his limits and keep himself vivid. In recent years, some observers have questioned whether he was taking up subjects rich and deserving enough of his abilities. Dwight Garner in his review of *The Noble Hustle* (the poker book), vividly praised Whitehead's talent—"You could point him at anything—a carwash, a bake sale, the cleaning of snot from a toddler's face—and I'd probably line up to read his account"—while making it very clear he felt it was being wasted. Garner called the book "a throwaway, a bluff, a large bet on a small hand," and questioned the sincerity of the undertaking: "you can sense that he's half embarrassed to be writing it."

As if to answer that criticism, Whitehead's new novel, *The Underground Railroad*, pursues perhaps the most formidable challenge of all: taking readers through "the blood-stained gate," as Frederick Douglass called it, onto the historical ground of American slavery. The uncompromising result is at once dazzling and disorienting, the work of a writer flexing, firing on all cylinders.

During a recent conversation at an Italian café in the West Village, Whitehead at times seemed slightly distracted. It's clear he does not enjoy talking about himself. He has always been highly skeptical of confessional modes. When he gives public talks, he likes to tell the audience he was born poor in the South—and then reveal he's just quoting Steve Martin from *The Jerk* (in which Martin plays a white man who believes he is born to a family of black sharecroppers). "I never liked Holden Caufield, *The Catcher in the*

Rye," he declares with a wink in his eye, in a promotional video for his most autobiographical book, *Sag Harbor*. "I feel like if he'd just been given some Prozac or an Xbox, it would have been a much shorter book, and a much better book."

In person, this stance becomes a kind of awkward warmth, even nerdiness: the eccentricity of the "blithely gifted," to borrow John Updike's 2001 assessment of "the young African American writer to watch." In dark blue jeans, his dreadlocks draping over a crisp white shirt, his glance slightly diffident behind neat glasses, Colson Whitehead is unmistakably a New Yorker—from Manhattan. He speaks in the native tongue—a streetwise blend of ironic nonchalance and snappy precision, a jolting rhythm not unlike that of the subway, always with an eye towards the next stop.

Whitehead was born in New York City and grew up mostly on the Upper West Side. He lives in Brooklyn now but recalls Manhattan with affection. "I like how Broadway gets really wide up there, how close the Hudson is," he says. "I'd live up there again if I could afford it." Asked what it was like growing up, *back in the day*, he brushes off the perceived roughness of that era: "New York was pretty run-down in the seventies and eighties, but if you think that's what a city looks like because you don't know anything else, then it seems normal. When I got out of college, I lived in the East Village and on cracked-out blocks in Brooklyn, and that seemed pretty normal, too."

He paints a picture of a loving and kind of average household. He was always surrounded by readers. "My mother reads a lot, and I had two older sisters, so their hand-me-down libraries were always around. I didn't need to be pushed." In a rare autobiographical essay, "A Psychotronic Childhood," he has described how this period of his life was deeply saturated by television, comics, and the "slasher" and "splatter" flicks, then in vogue, that he watched in New York's B-movie theaters. A self-described shut-in, he "preferred to lie on the living-room carpet, watching horror movies," where one could acquire "an education on the subjects of sapphic vampires and ill-considered head transplants" while snacking "on Oscar Mayer baloney, which I rolled into cigarette-size payloads of processed meat." Unsurprisingly, he read "a lot of commercial fiction, Stephen King—the first thick (to me) book I read was in fifth grade, King's *Night Shift*. I read that over and over." His early literary ambitions, he has said, were simple: "Put 'the black' in front of [the title of] every Stephen King novel, that's what I wanted to do."

After graduating from Trinity School, Whitehead entered Harvard. It was the late 1980s, and the way he tells it makes it sound like he was a poster boy for Gen X slackerdom. (The archetype must feel almost quaint to the hypernetworking Zuckerberg generation.) It's not that he didn't enjoy his time at Harvard—he did attend his twenty-fifth reunion, he informed me—but he seems to have been determined not to try too hard to be involved in anything or to stand out in any way. He read in his room a lot, he says, absorbing a wide range of things. But it was the way he was absorbing these strains that is most revealing: "I think it helped that for my first exposure to Beckett I took it to be a form of high realism. A guy is buried up to his neck in sand and can't move; he has an itch on his leg he can't scratch. That sounds like Monday morning to me." (Responding to the suggestion that his novels suggest the influence of Ralph Ellison and Thomas Pynchon, Whitehead is noncommittal but open to the idea: "What excited me about writers like Ellison and Pynchon was the way you could use fantasy and still get at social and political themes," he says. "That was very revealing to me . . . like here's this serious book on race, but it has all this wild stuff in it.")

At Harvard, Whitehead played the role of young aspiring writer the way he imagined it. The results were not necessarily promising. "I considered myself a writer, but I didn't actually write anything," he says. "I wore black and smoked cigarettes, but I didn't actually sit down and write, which apparently is part of the process of writing." He applied to creative-writing seminars twice—and failed to get in both times.

The most important undergraduate legacy has been his lasting friendship with Kevin Young, an aspiring, charismatic poet from Kansas who was already involved with the Dark Room Collective, a gathering of young black writers that has played a major role in shaping contemporary poetry during the past two decades. Whitehead, never more than peripherally involved, says, "Kevin was always more serious than I was. He already knew where he was going, what he was about. . . . I wasn't much of a team player."

After graduation, Whitehead gravitated back to New York City. He went to work at the *Village Voice*, writing album reviews and television criticism. He soon mastered the magazine's signature downtown stir-fry of pop-culture fluency, melding high- and lowbrow, theory and snark, punk and hip hop: an inevitable rite of passage, given his influences. "I came up in the seventies and eighties reading *CREEM* ["America's Only Rock 'n' Roll Magazine"], stuff like that, so I knew pretty early on that I wanted to be involved in that scene," he says. Working in the book section at the *Voice*, he says "was where I learned how to be a writer."

That writer debuted in 1999 to instant acclaim with the disquieting *The Intuitionist*, set in an unspecified midcentury Gotham, a noir metropolis straight out of Jules Dassin and Fritz Lang. In its conceit, the world of elevator inspectors is divided between rival schools: Empiricists, who work by collecting data and making methodical observations, and Intuitionists, a minority of gifted inspectors who have a second sight that allows them to read elevator mechanics intuitively—an ability scorned and feared by the dominant faction. The novel follows Lila Mae Watson, a member of the Department of Elevator Inspectors, as she tries to solve the case of a suspicious crash and also untangle the mysterious aphorisms of one James Fulton, whose gnomic text, *Theoretical Elevators*, may provide clues to a secret about its author and the nature of Intuitionism itself. It's impossible not to like Lila Mae, a black woman occupying a role stereotypically identified with the square-jawed private eye, who uses her cool and wits to navigate this murky underworld and stay one step ahead of the men trying to frame her. Part of the fun is in the writing itself. Whitehead's prose oscillates playfully between the pulpy, telegraphic neonoir à la James Ellroy and the allegorical ruminations of Ralph Ellison's *Invisible Man*.

This gives the novel a slippery feeling, a cool detachment that makes it easier to admire than to love. It's as though Whitehead built that book on the principles of stealth technology, every facet rigorously designed to achieve what it is also about: a game of camouflage and detection, the irony of invisibility in plain sight. His interest in unstable visibility suggests the theme of racial passing, a concern with a long history in the African American novel. As the scholar Michele Elam pointed out, *The Intuitionist* can be read as "a passing novel in both form and content." The familiar hard-boiled detective plot turns out to be merely a lure, a skin-thin surface masking a speculative novel of ideas.

As a first novel, *The Intuitionist* registered as a shot across the bow, as though Whitehead were daring readers to box him in. It was also a first glimpse of what has since become something of an authorial signature: an ironic deployment of genre as a mask for an eccentric but also cutting vision of American culture. It's an approach that can remind one of Thomas Pynchon in novels like *The Crying of Lot 49* (critics have compared its heroine Oedipa Maas to Lila Mae Watson) and *Inherent Vice*, or to the filmmaking of the Coen brothers, with their affectionate but sinister parodies of Hollywood noir in *Barton Fink* or *Fargo*. Like them, Whitehead delights in recasting the iconography of Americana, troubling its conventions and clichés by pressing them to their limits, and releasing that energy in the form of bleak satire and an impassive attitude toward violence.

In 2008, novelist Charles Johnson published an essay in the *American Scholar* titled "The End of the Black Narrative," in which he argued that the history of slavery in America had become a crutch for understanding any and all experiences of black life—that at the dawn of the twenty-first century it had "outlived its usefulness as a tool of interpretation" and should be discarded in favor of "new and better stories, new concepts, and new vocabularies and grammar based not on the past but on the dangerous, exciting, and unexplored present." It's an argument that has analogs in academic circles as well, where a movement around "afro-pessimism" has prompted debates in recent years over whether contemporary black life can ever transcend the historical experience of slavery. Whitehead hasn't read the essay, but he says the argument makes sense to him if it means black writers need to have the freedom to write whatever and however they want. (He resists attempts to theorize his own work, and it's clear he's fairly allergic to the scholarly efforts to categorize his literature. He's an excellent parodist and, whether aiming his wit at the sophistications of academic vernacular or the flummery of marketing lingo, he's a master at deconstructing jargons. He once opened a talk at the Du Bois Institute at Harvard by delivering a compelling close reading of Flavor Flav's "Can't Do Nuttin for Ya Man" at the lectern.)

Yet his work has been viewed along these lines. His 2009 coming-of-age novel, *Sag Harbor*, follows a group of "bougie" black kids as they try to survive the summer of 1985 in the black enclave their parents have carved out in the Hamptons. A good part of the comedy revolves around the ways the main character, Benji Cooper, and his friends try and fail to act "authentically black": city boys with toy BB guns awkwardly grasping at gangsta status. Reviewing the novel, journalist and cultural critic Touré, known for popularizing the term "post-blackness," inducted Whitehead into a constellation of figures opening up the scripts of blackness: "now Kanye, Questlove, Santigold, Zadie Smith, and Colson Whitehead can do blackness their way without fear of being branded pseudo or incognegro," he declared.

"Post-blackness" should not be confused with the "postracial." "We'll be postracial when we're all dead," Whitehead quips, alluding to *Zone One*, in which his hero, an Everyman nicknamed Mark Spitz, is part of a sweeper unit clearing out the undead in postapocalyptic downtown Manhattan. In fact, no one has more deliciously julienned this particular bit of cant. In a 2009 *New York Times* essay, "The Year of Living Postracially," Whitehead offered himself to the Obama administration as a "secretary of postracial affairs," who like the hero of his 2006 novel *Apex Hides the Hurt*, will rebrand cultural artifacts to meet new societal standards. "*Diff'rent Strokes* and *What's Happening!!* will now be known as *Different Strokes* and *What Is Happening*?" he suggested, and Spike Lee's *Do the Right Thing* would be recast with "multicultural Brooklyn writers—subletting realists, couch-surfing postmodernists, landlords whose métier is haiku—getting together on a mildly hot summer afternoon, not too humid, to host a block party, the proceeds of which go to a charity for restless leg syndrome . . ." The essay suggests the influence of Ishmael Reed, whose hallucinatory satires mine the absurdities of racism for comic effect, highlighting how their surreal and grotesque contortions are refracted in language and sublimated in collective phantasmagorias: television shows, music videos, and the movies.

The critic James Wood has complained about a "filmic" quality in Whitehead's writing. It is undeniable—but younger readers may find that that quality is its own kind of literacy, a clear picture where Wood sees only static. Rightly or not, there is something contemporary and vivid in Whitehead's direct apprehension of the way lives are overdetermined and bound by chains of mediated images. It's a gambit that has surfaced as a question for the contemporary novel before: David Foster Wallace famously worried that television had repurposed irony to commercial ends, defanging it as a weapon in fiction. Whitehead has drawn just the opposite lesson, wagering that irony not only sustains the postmodern novel—but that it can even deepen the stain of allegory.

Can this ironic method successfully take on American slavery? It might seem intimidating, perhaps even overwhelming, to write about a subject where the stakes feel so high. In recent years, the history of slavery, never far from the surface of American life, has seeped back into popular consciousness with renewed urgency. On television, *Underground*, which debuted this spring, follows the fugitive slave trail; and this past spring the History Channel remade *Roots*, the groundbreaking 1977 miniseries based on Alex Haley's novel. On film, black directors are also thrusting slavery to the fore, notably Steve McQueen in *12 Years a Slave* and now Nate Parker's *The Birth of a Nation*, about Nat Turner's rebellion. This year has also brought at least two other novels that will frame the reception of Whitehead's: Yaa Gyasi's *Homegoing* reconsiders how African identities interlock but also diverge from the "black narrative"; Ben H. Winters's *Underground Airlines* imagines a counterfactual history in which the Civil War never took place and bounty hunters roam a contemporary United States seeking runaways. And all this still pales before the inevitable comparisons with major writers on the same theme. Whitehead anticipates these questions, and instantly brushes aside comparisons. "You have to do your own thing, right? Morrison"—that's Toni Morrison—"already wrote *Beloved*; you're not going to compete with that. I have to write the book that makes sense to me, that's entirely my own vision."

The Underground Railroad follows Cora, a slave on a cotton plantation in Georgia, as she makes a break for freedom. She becomes a runaway, a "passenger" who must elude capture as she makes her way northward on the famous Underground Railroad—in Whitehead's conceit, made literal rather than metaphorical. "When I was a kid I always thought it was a real railroad," he says with a flashing grin. It's a testament to the power of metaphor, and, like the ghost in Morrison's *Beloved* that haunts the former slaves of Sweet Home plantation even as they try to re-create their new lives in freedom, it marks an assertion of the novelist's supreme freedom: the freedom that allows fiction to breathe and stand on its own, and writers to carve out a personal dimension within material fraught with communal and ideological strictures.

If *The Underground Railroad* seems to give in to the inescapable pull of "the black narrative" which Whitehead had been celebrated for evading, the new novel isn't as new it may appear. "This project has been on my mind for at least ten years," Whitehead says. "I started thinking about it around the time I was doing *John Henry Days*, but I set it aside. I didn't feel like I was ready yet to tackle it, the way I was writing then . . . I'm much more into concision now in my writing, and I think this book needed that."

For it, Whitehead did a good deal of research—looking to Eric Foner's *Gateway to Freedom* to depict the cat-and-mouse game between slavecatchers and freemen scouting for runaways along the docks of New York harbor, and reading the Works Progress Administration's collection of slave narratives for material details of slave life. But above all, Whitehead drew on the rich literary history to which he is adding a new chapter, refashioning famous scenes in Harriet Beecher Stowe's *Uncle Tom's Cabin* and Harriet Jacobs's *Incidents in the Life of a Slave Girl*—especially her account of seven years spent hiding in an attic (a passage he singled out as having profoundly marked him when he read it in college). The ominous figure of the slavecatcher Ridgeway suggests more recent antecedents. Cormac McCarthy's *Blood Meridian*, with its vision of bounty hunters chasing scalps on an American frontier steeped in apocalyptic gore, echoes in Whitehead's chronicling of the orgiastic violence that haunts the hunting grounds of slavery.

The novel explicitly links slavery to the engine of global capitalism. The theme has gained prominence in recent years, notably through works like *River of Dark Dreams: Slavery and Empire in the Cotton Kingdom* by Walter Johnson and *Empire of Cotton: A Global History* by Sven Beckert (both of Harvard's history department), which have enlarged the context for our understanding of slavery and resuscitated neglected arguments put forth at least a generation earlier by black Marxists like Eric Williams and Cedric

Robinson. The idea of a capitalist drive behind slavery always seemed intuitive to Whitehead, he says. "Being from New York," he suggests, "you can see the drive for exploitation all around you. It just always seemed obvious to me."

Rather than centering on one site or aspect of slavery, *The Underground Railroad* presents readers with a kind of composite. The novel proceeds episodically, with each stage of Cora's voyage presenting a variation on the conditions of enslavement and emancipation. Caesar, a fellow slave on the Randall plantation who encourages Cora to run away with him, compares their predicament to that of Gulliver, whose book of travels his more lenient master has allowed him to read. He foresees a flight "from one troublesome island to the next, never recognizing where he was, until the world ran out." This sense of variation on a theme—with no exit in sight—creates a sense of blind forward propulsion without "progress": scenes of medical experimentation that recall the infamous Tuskegee Syphilis Studies appear side by side with those of coffles, auction blocks, abolitionist safe houses, as well as the vision of Valentine farm, a haven in Indiana founded by a successful mixed-race free black who believes that hard work and exposure to high culture will secure the acceptance of his white neighbors. "I wanted to get away from the typical, straightforward plantation," Whitehead says. His novel doesn't seek to reenact history, but rather to imagine and represent simultaneously the many hydra heads of a system designed to perpetuate the enclosure and domination of human beings.

The genre of fugitive-slave narratives has long been haunted by sentimentality. As the scholar Saidiya Hartman has suggested, the use of the pain of others for readers' own purification or enlightenment—or at worst, entertainment—is a deep problem for this genre. Many have argued that the truth of slavery can only be understood first-hand. William Wells Brown, who published an account of his own escape to freedom in 1847, famously asserted that "Slavery has never been represented; Slavery never can be represented."

To write about slavery is to face head-on this risk of representation. *The Underground Railroad* can feel at times overrepresented, almost too explanatory—seeking at every turn to demonstrate how this or that aspect of slavery worked, flagging a character's motivations by relating them back to that system. There's precious little room for characters to be something other than what they appear to be, something more than allegorical props. At one point, Cora, staying at a temporary haven in South Carolina, goes up to the rooftop to look out over the town and up at the sky. The scene's only function seems to be to give the reader a chance to overhear some of her thoughts and hopes, something of who she is when she is not engaged in the business of trying to stay alive. Despite Whitehead's best efforts, Cora remains sketched rather than known, a specter seen through a glass darkly. She is a Gothic woman in the attic, haunting the national consciousness, a symbol more than a person. It's a connection Whitehead makes explicit: "Now that she had run away and seen a bit of the country, Cora wasn't sure the Declaration described anything real at all," says his narrator. "America was a ghost in the darkness, like her."

Yet there is something new and perhaps unprecedented in the way Whitehead has reasserted the agency of black writers to reconstruct "the black narrative" from within. Whitehead interleaves *The Underground Railroad* with invented runaway-slave advertisements by planters seeking to recover their property. But in the last one, the hand of the author and that of his protagonist are momentarily overlaid, as though we are reading an advertisement Cora has left us, "written by herself," as the subtitles of slave narratives habitually put it. "Ran Away," reads the title and declares below: "She was never property." The device harnesses the power of fiction to assert impossible authorship, to thrust into view the voice that could not have spoken—but speaks nonetheless. Cora becomes, in the last instance, a mirror not only for the drama of slavery, but for the whole problem of *writing* about slavery: a vector that points away from something unspeakable and toward something unknown—and perhaps unknowable.

Interestingly, *John Henry Days*, the book by Whitehead that deals most substantially with the history of black America, is also almost certainly his least read. Its hero, J. Sutter, is a freelance writer drawn from New York to an assignment in Talcott, West Virginia: the US Postal Service is hosting a festival celebrating a new John Henry commemorative stamp. Whitehead uses the mythical man and J. Sutter's pursuit of his meaning to transect the sediment layers of black history. His novel starts at the surface of a media-frenzied America circa 1996, simmering with racial unease and tortuous political correctness, then tunnels down to the labor of steel-driving gangs in the 1870s. Along the way, it stops to recast figures like Paul Robeson or rewrite the rioting at Altamont Speedway. Suggesting another history, or set of histories, behind the one we think we know, Whitehead poses the thorny problem of how to interpret the stories we inherit.

In *The Grey Album*, his collection of essays on black aesthetics, Whitehead's friend Kevin Young has advanced the idea of the "shadow book"—certain texts which, for a variety of reasons, may fail to turn up: because they were never written, because they are only implied within other texts, or simply because they have been lost. One might add to this a category of books that are *eclipsed*. For *John Henry Days*, it was *Infinite Jest*. Both are postmodern leviathans, ambitiously unwieldy and bursting with insight, indelibly products of the 1990s. Yet Whitehead's book has never acquired the kind of cult following that David Foster Wallace's has. Published in 2001, it seems to have been eclipsed at least in part by historical events (though it can't have helped that Jonathan Franzen wrote a self-absorbed review for the *New York Times* that ignored any discussion of race, a stupefying lacuna; Whitehead says that Franzen in fact later apologized for it). If *John Henry Days* is the "shadow book" of the nineties, the other great masterpiece behind the masterpiece everyone knows, it is also a powerful complement to this new novel on slavery. In time it may be recognized that these books are among Whitehead's defining achievements, capturing the black experience in America with a wide-angle lens, carrying both its mythic and realistic truth, and delivering it over the transom into the maw of our digitally mediated Internet age.

In the meantime, with *The Underground Railroad* gone to press, Whitehead has been catching up on the reading he loves. He's reading a lot of crime fiction, Kelly Link's short stories, and he's well into the latest Marlon James novel. His daughter is an avid reader of comics, so he's catching up on those as well. Asked what he might work on next, he answers that he's still focused on promoting the new book, of course—but possibly something about Harlem, something set in the 1960s. After lunch wraps up, he heads down the block, walking smoothly, smoking a cigarette, back into the thrumming heart of the city.

"You are a New Yorker when what was there before is more real and solid than what is here now," Whitehead writes in the opening pages of *The Colossus of New York*. A strain of apocalyptic foreboding, tempered by a refusal to sentimentalize trauma, courses through Colson Whitehead's fiction. It's present in the books he wrote even before 9/11. But the attacks of that day inevitably cloud the lyrical essays gathered in *Colossus*, a collection published in 2001, a time of disaster and mourning in the place he has always called home.

Yet unlike so much writing about New York, Whitehead's deliberately shies away from emphasizing what makes it special and unique. Whitehead writes instead of the invisible cities that everyone knows and carries within memory, not necessarily the ones that still exist in brick and mortar. He writes about the universal qualities of arrival and departure, loneliness and haste. His second-person address to "you" contains within it the gentle pressure of Walt Whitman's "I too," from "Crossing Brooklyn Ferry."

Whitehead's answer to the calamity of terrorism is to insist, like Whitman, on the unbreakable power of the city to transform the vulnerability of the huddled crowd into a heightened, even universal empathy.

"Talking about New York is a way of talking about the world," Whitehead writes on the last page. True, but it is also a way of reflecting the world through one's own experience of it. It seems not entirely a coincidence that elevators and underground trains, two of New York's most iconic modes of transportation, are the symbolic vehicles Whitehead has invoked as he grapples with the wider meanings of America. Whether he is writing about the city he knows best or the lives of characters in almost unimaginable circumstances, Whitehead has demonstrated time and again a remarkable capacity for turning what appear to be evasions into encounters, the historical arc we want to hide from into the narrative arc we can't avoid. He is a writer who stands squarely in our present dilemmas and confusions, and suggests lines of sight no one else seems to have considered or dared to imagine.

"If You Don't Have Hope, Then Why Go On?": An Interview with Colson Whitehead

Vicky Mochama / 2016

From *Hazlitt Magazine*, September 12, 2016. Reprinted with permission of Vicky Mochama.

Colson Whitehead's new novel, *The Underground Railroad*, tells the story of Cora, a girl born into slavery, as she escapes from the plantation with Caesar, a new friend and fellow escapee, while Ridgeway, a slave patroller, obsessively dogs her in pursuit as she makes her way along the titular tracks. Whitehead takes the slave narrative to new territory, however, by answering the question: What if the Underground Railroad was a real railroad?

Station masters offer help and guidance at stops along the way. Lumbly, a conductor on her first train, tells the pair that "[every] state is different. Each is a state of possibility, with its own customs and way of doing things. Moving through them, you'll see the breadth of the country before you reach your final stop." Whitehead's story takes Cora through several American states as each one grapples with slavery's presence and legacy. And in each, she experiences that state of possibility—not just of what America is and what it could be, but also who she is and who she can be.

It is a beautiful, jarring, and compelling story—no surprise that it has quickly become one of the most talked about books of the year. Among its many accolades, including making its way onto President Obama's summer reading list, it's an Oprah Book Club selection. It was illegal to teach slaves to read and those slaves who could risked their lives; in the novel, Cora values deeply the ability to read and learn. I can't help but be struck that we're in a moment in time in which a black woman is such an influential player in the literary world.

I spoke with Colson Whitehead by phone.

Vicky Mochama: I want to start at the end of the book. In the acknowledgments, you cite Prince, Sonic Youth, and David Bowie. What role did music play in writing this book?

Colson Whitehead: [*laughs*] I started writing fiction about twenty years ago. When I work I play a loop of my favorite two hundred songs on a playlist. It goes from the Ramones to David Bowie to the Lounge Lizards. Whenever I finish a book and I get to the last day of writing the first draft and I only have two pages to go, I put on [Prince's] *Purple Rain* and [Sonic Youth's] *Daydream Nation*. That's my ritual. Whenever I put those albums on back to back, I know I'm in the home stretch.

VM: What was it like for you to this year lose those artists that were fundamental to your process?

CW: I guess you never contemplate Bowie gone. And then I did the acknowledgments and Prince passed away. There's always the music. It's a great loss. When Bowie died, I played my children (who are two and eleven years old) loops of his old music videos. Now, when I take my son into bed, I have to play him "Silent Night" and "Ashes to Ashes" by David Bowie, so I end up singing it every day. One day he'll ask what a junkie is because that's one of the lines in "Ashes to Ashes," and I'm not sure what I'll say. But we'll get there.

VM: Talking of your process, when did you sit down and think you could actually write this book?

CW: I had the idea sixteen years ago and didn't feel ready. I came up with the premise of exploring that childhood notion that the Underground Railroad is an actual subway. I kept putting it off. I didn't want to tackle the enormity of slavery. I didn't feel emotionally ready, and I didn't feel mature enough as a person. As a writer, it seemed very daunting. Every couple of years, I'd go back to my notes and think, Am I ready? And the answer was always, No. But finally, about two years ago, it seemed I was afraid of doing this book, and it was time to confront why and just take the plunge.

VM: What did you find out?

CW: We walk around with different ideas of what slavery was. But to actually read the testimonials from former slaves and hundreds of slave narratives, there's no escaping the brutality of the system, and, in my case, what my ancestors went through. It was a consideration of who in my family didn't make it out.

VM: I think as black writers there's always a sense that we don't want to talk about the things that are meant to define our communities. Did you have any doubts about writing a slavery book?

CW: Mostly in terms of ability and wanting to do the idea justice. It had a lot of possibilities in the premise of the book, so I waited until I was ready. The hardest part was once I'd done the research and realized how many terrors I'd have to submit my protagonist and her friends to—that seemed very hard. The reality is that in the book she's sixteen years old, and by that time she's probably suffered some form of sexual assault or one of the terrors of slavery. So having to put everybody through the horrors of that first chapter was difficult to contemplate.

VM: The book extends the childhood notion that the Underground Railroad is possibly a real railroad. I was talking to my sister about this, and she said for a very long time, even as an adult, she thought there were real trains.

CW: It's a fairly common mistake that people make when they're young. If you search for "the Underground Railroad" on Twitter, high school kids are making fun of friends, saying, "Sarah thinks the Underground Railroad is a real railroad smh." The image is very powerful and informs our idea of how things work.

VM: What was your research process for the book?

CW: I tried to do enough research to get going. In this case, there are a few histories of the Underground Railroad. The one that I came to first that was most useful was called *Bound for Canaan* by Fergus Bordewich, and that was very comprehensive. And really, just slave narratives. There are the big ones: Harriet Tubman, Frederick Douglass—Harriet Jacobs, who spent seven years in an attic, informed the North Carolina section. The US government during the Depression hired writers to get people back to work, and the writers interviewed former slaves: eighty-year-old, ninety-year-old people who'd been on the plantation when they were kids and teens. Some of the accounts are just three paragraphs and are about farming life. Some are ten pages long and contain someone's whole biography. There's hundreds and hundreds of them. I was able to get a log of details about people living in different plantations in Tennessee versus Georgia versus Florida, sugar versus cotton. It was my introduction to the variety of the slave experience. As a writer, it was just a really rich source of material.

VM: How does it feel having done all this research in order to write the book and then to see people take issue with statements like Michelle Obama saying slaves built the White House?

CW: I'm fairly well-educated, and the true scope of the depravity of slavery was unknown to me. I hadn't thought about it in a while. The research really opened my eyes. In terms of the reaction to Michelle Obama, I don't think we teach the truth of slavery. I don't think we teach in our schools a tenth of the reality. In general, we skip to the Civil War and Lincoln and then slavery was done. We don't talk about Reconstruction or Jim Crow. We fast-forward to *Brown v. Board of Education*, which ended segregated schools; we go to Martin Luther King. In schools, we skip to the good parts. Most people are coming from a place of ignorance. But also, who wants to talk about their great-grandparents' culpability? Who wants to talk about how their great-great-grandparents were abused? It's a natural reaction to shy away from the true horror of it. I'm not excusing it, but it is a lot for the mind to handle on top of our ignorance and not wanting to think about the past.

VM: Did you write this book to explore how you felt or understood slavery?

CW: Not so much slavery, but slavery and American history and this character. I think all books are an exploration of the world in different ways and trying to figure out how the world works. The Underground Railroad, because of its structure, allowed me to talk about different aspects and phases in black American history—whether it was the Tuskegee syphilis experiments, which make an appearance, the commonality of the immigrant experience and the despised other, whether you're hated for your blackness or your Irishness or your Italianness. Certain books allow me to discover how I feel about things, and then there are other books that allow me to make sense of how the world has come to be what it is.

VM: A couple of the characters express the idea that if God didn't want the Africans to be slaves, then they wouldn't be. I feel like that's an idea you see currently in many different ways. Were there moments that you could see contemporary life reflecting things that you were writing in the book?

CW: There's a policy called Stop and Frisk in New York City which allowed any cop to stop anyone and on the barest pretext search them and check for ID. It's had different names over the years. It's an echo of early police enforcement during slave times—there was no police force, and the people who stepped in to keep order were the slave patrollers. They could stop a black person, go into any black person's home—whether it was on the plantation or a free person's house—and demand to see their papers. Those kinds of parallels aren't hard to force into the book. The world was pretty racist a hundred and fifty years ago, and it's pretty racist now.

VM: One of the books that Caesar reads is actually *Gulliver's Travels*. Was it intentional that the book would mirror that kind of a road trip?

CW: When I first came up with the idea that each state would be a different state of possibility, the immediate comparison is *Gulliver's Travels*. I'm not a Jonathan Swift fanatic, but that structure became a convenient way to talk about the book with other people. It is an episodic adventure story in a certain kind of a way: it's *The Odyssey*, *Pilgrim's Progress*, *Gulliver's Travels*, so that structure was an early decision I made and allowed me a lot of creative play.

VM: The character of Ridgeway is reflective of an attitude held by poor whites—

CW: —and rich whites. He's a voice for the American philosophy of "might makes right," "if you can keep it, it's yours," and, "if you can't keep it, why not destroy it?" It's an imperial philosophy that plays out around the world and in different phases of history even today.

VM: At one point, he elaborates on his theory of the system, and as you're listening to him explain it the logic starts to fall apart a bit, but he says, "It's an imperative I have to refuse"—that imperative being to allow the system to break down. Is that at the heart of the difficulty of addressing racism now?

CW: I think you want to preserve your power. If you talk to a lot of Trump supporters, they're upset that people of color and women are in power, and white men have lost their stranglehold on possibility. When you have something good going, you definitely want to protect it. That's definitely what Ridgeway fears. That's what people in contemporary America fear: what place they have in the future when the people they've subjugated for centuries are coming into their own.

VM: So what do you envision when it comes to America's future in dealing with one of its original sins?

CW: I think things improve and progress quite slowly. Certainly, I never thought we'd have a black president. For most of my life, that seemed inconceivable. For some people, it seems inconceivable that we'll have a female president. Growing up with Margaret Thatcher [*laughs*] it didn't seem that impossible. I have two kids who don't think it's odd at all that we have a black male president and a female candidate, so that is obviously an advancement. I can vote. I can publish; obviously, I'm not living under the yoke of slavery. Things improve slowly—not fast enough because old systems die hard but I certainly have the hope that my children and their generation are moving into a better world. Cora, when she takes that first fateful step off the plantation, believes that there's a better world out there. If you don't have hope, then why go on?

#ScribdChat with Colson Whitehead

Michael Cohen / 2016

From the *Literally* blog on *Scribd.com*, October 12, 2016. Reprinted with permission.

Colson Whitehead's latest novel, *The Underground Railroad*, was published this summer to rave reviews from columnists, Oprah, and even President Obama. The Scribd editorial team quickly fell under the spell of the ambitious, expansive, and important novel, as well. So when we heard that Whitehead would be traveling through San Francisco on his book tour, we invited him to join us for a #ScribdChat and were thrilled when he graciously agreed. Given the story's historical and sociological themes, we invited Professor Michael Cohen, of the African American Studies Department at the University of California, Berkeley, to conduct the interview. What followed was a fascinating discussion of history, literary theory, contemporary race relations, and what it's like to join the pantheon of Oprah's Book Club authors.

Michael Cohen: I wanted you to know that I told my class of two hundred students at UC Berkeley that if a better novel was published this year I would eat that novel in front of them, and I think it's a safe bet on my part. But speaking of bets here, your last book on poker, *The Noble Hustle*, portrays a character named Colson Whitehead who suffers from all sorts of self-afflicted maladies and imaginary failures, and I'm wondering how this character might feel when it becomes apparent that his new book is about to become a huge hit after being endorsed by President Obama, Oprah Winfrey, and, perhaps most importantly, Michiko Kakutani.

Colson Whitehead: It's been a very wild six weeks. I'm in a good mood, it's all very surprising, and being in a good mood seems to be working. This is my eighth book, and it doesn't always go like this. Sometimes critics understand what you're trying to do, sometimes they don't, and sometimes people take a chance and pick up your book. When it happens like this, you have to go with it, so I've been a very happy boy the past few weeks.

MC: I'm interested to hear what you think of the Oprah Winfrey endorsement. Is there any temptation to go all Jonathan Franzen on her and say, "Well, you know, this popularity in book club sales is really going to damage my reputation as a starving artist."

CW: Well, I mean, you're in the same company as Toni Morrison, Cormac McCarthy, and William Faulkner, so those guys aren't too shabby. So I was really excited. You know, my books can have oddball premises. Not everyone is down for a book that is about an elevator inspector, not everyone likes zombies.

What Oprah does is helps me jump the barrier to people who might not pick up my work.

MC: Has writing gotten any easier for you over the years?

CW: I don't worry about finishing the book; I know it will get done. It may be painful, but it always gets done in the end. I like to make jokes about how hard it is, and it is difficult. Especially with this book I remember the days when I figured out this or that, about Cora, about her mother, and you have to remember the real days of victory when you write a book. It's those days when something happens and you make a new kind of sentence for yourself that you haven't done before, or you figure out a way to plot something that's more efficient that you've done in the past.

There's a lot of drudgery, but there're also these really fun moments when you've made a new leap or figured out something about the book that's important, and that stays with you also.

MC: Now that you've obtained this new stage, would you consider writing comic books? And if Marvel or DC were to come to you tomorrow, what character would you want to write?

CW: Like a lot of people my age, I was inspired to become a writer by reading science fiction and horror and, of course, comic books—late seventies Marvel, and all of those runs on the *X-Men* that are now made into movies, and I think at my age most novelists wanted to write the *X-Men* or be in the *X-Men*. It's kind of a generational thread.

And I have been asked a few times, but whenever I try to get out of my form and do a film or a comic it always seems like a lot of work; it seems really hard. I think, in between things, that I can teach or write a screenplay and then after about ten days I think, I'll just write a novel; this is really hard.

MC: Let's turn to the book for a moment. I was wondering if you could give us a sort of "back of the cover" description of the text itself, as offered by the author himself.

CW: Sure, well, it's about the Underground Railroad. I like to be direct. It's about a young woman named Cora; she's about sixteen or seventeen. It's not clear how old she is because slave masters didn't keep track of how old their slaves were. They moved around a lot, and in the same way you might not know if your dog Spot is six or seven or what his birthday is, that's how slave masters saw their property. So she's on a plantation in Georgia, and she's a stray in the parlance of the plantation. She has no family, her mother has run off years before, and a new slave comes to the plantation and plants the idea that maybe they can avail themselves of the Underground Railroad and escape.

And in this book the Underground Railroad is an actual network of tracks below America. I think I'm not alone in that when I first heard about it, when I was in the fourth or fifth grade, I envisioned a subway beneath the Earth. And then you find out, if you have a good teacher, it's not. So I was thinking, what if it were a literal network? That's the premise, but it's not the story.

I added this other complication in that in every state our hero goes to as she runs North, it's a different state of American possibility, sort of like *Gulliver's Travels*. So the book is being rebooted every sixty pages as she enters a new state that presents an alternative view of American history of what might have happened if we had gone differently.

MC: I really felt the powerful pacing of the novel; it moves very deliberately and quickly. I felt that the book contains so much more than its 306 pages. It's a quick read; I really felt the narrative drive. But there are worlds within this, and in a sense it strikes me as a triumph of style. Can you talk about how you arrived at the tone, the narrative voice that this book offered?

CW: In general, in my previous books, it takes about a hundred pages for the narrative voice to come together. Is the narrator someone who likes long sentences or short sentences—big, five-clause pile-ups—or are they more direct; is it first-person or third-person? But for the first time the voice clicked very quickly in the first six pages. I open up with a six-page biographical sketch of Cora's mother. It follows her from when she's abducted from Western Africa and she comes to various plantations in the US, and the voice just came really quickly. Usually when you arrive at the voice you have to go back and retrofit everything that's come before. But the kind of matter-of-fact nature of the narrator in the face of all this brutality, and these odd events, the narrator tells a story that seems to fit. I think it came partially from the slave narrative that I used as research.

In the 1930s, FDR during the Great Depression wanted to get people back to work, so he sent out writers to interview former slaves, people who were kids or teenagers at the time of slavery. Some of the accounts are about farming, others are about master and slave relationships, but a lot of them are very matter-of-fact. They just say things like "my mother was sold off and the next day I was picking," and there's a whole universe in that sentence. But they seem very removed from it, and while the book does get fantastic, I wanted a first section to take place in Georgia and be as realistic as I can do it.

In delivering a lot of the brutality in that section, the matter-of-fact tone seemed to be effective in terms of bringing the reader in.

MC: In the acknowledgments of the book you mention Nathan Huggins and Stephen Jay Gould, and I was wondering if you have ever taken any classes from these men at Harvard.

CW: I did. I wasn't the type of person to know my professor; I was always in the back row. But my first semester in 1987, as a freshman, I took a class called "Changing Concepts of Race in America," and it was Nathan Huggins and Stephen Jay Gould. It was my awakening as an African American to my history, and it stayed with me. I ended up using a lot of what we talked about in the class in the book.

MC: It raises the question, just how far back in your career as a writer does this text actually go?

CW: There's a section about the Tuskegee Syphilis Experiment, and we had a few classes on that, read the book *Bad Blood*. When I was a senior I started reading more slave narratives, including Harriet Jacobs. Harriet Jacobs was a woman who hit puberty, and her master had sexual designs on her. And she ran away and hid for seven years in an attic in North Carolina until she could get passage out.

How do you spend seven years in an attic? That story stayed with me, and in the North Carolina section in this book, I've taken part of that story to animate Cora's story.

MC: It is a remarkable reproduction of that; I mean the North Carolina section of the book is just horrifying. It suggests the question in reading this.

I've read before about your life-long love of horror movies. Obviously, *Zone One*, your previous novel is a zombie story set in New York, but this seems in some ways like a consolidation of a lifetime of wondering what horror movies would look like if black folks were the stumbling feminine protagonist and American history itself were the monster chasing them.

CW: The narrative of a slave escaped is full of danger and suspense, all of those moments when the white lady falls and has to get up. So you can't get any more-higher stakes than life or death, and the penalty for running away many times was death. So in organizing this story I definitely wanted to have those moments of adventure, those moments that are hair-raising. The material itself, I think, has that action suspense structure built into it.

MC: Did you give yourself a set of rules? Did you put limits on yourself in terms of thinking about how you created, as you call them, these "states of possibility"?

CW: First, it's not a historical novel. If you're making the Underground Railroad literal, then obviously you are departing from the truth of it. But having made that decision, it allowed me to play with time, so I could bring in the Tuskegee experiments. I could play with race laws from North Carolina and Oregon, and bring in the Holocaust.

So my rule was: I'm not sticking to the facts; I'm sticking to the truth. The truth of 1850 emanates much further into the present.

MC: This is a work that fits into a growing but none the less established genre, you know, when we talk about the neoslave narrative through Toni Morrison, Octavia Butler, or someone like Kara Walker. Did you find yourself embracing these artists as influences, or did you have to tune them out?

CW: I want to see what other people are doing, and sometimes I don't. It really depends on how I feel about the material. I want to reread *Beloved*; I hadn't read that in almost twenty-five years. I opened up *Beloved*, read about thirty-five pages, and thought, I'm totally screwed. You know, Toni Morrison, she's a genius, and eventually I had to stop reading.

No matter what you write, there's probably someone smarter and more talented than you who has written it before. All you can hope is that you have something to bring to the table and that you have your distinct point of view to add. So I don't worry about competing; I just hope that it's, if not in the top ten slavery novels, hopefully in the top twenty.

MC: It's interesting because all of these books have a touch of the fantastic. In a sense, you're in good hands. Were you ever tempted to write a comprehensively realistic novel about slavery?

CW: No, it never occurred to me. I think in terms of the most realistic. The most realistic section is the Georgia section, just to honor the slave dead, my nameless ancestors, and whoever lived and died in Georgia or Florida. The more research I did the more I knew that there weren't going to be a lot of jokes in this book, but I knew that even my satirical reserve, the distance I usually keep, I would not be able to keep up. So really, it does enter into fantastic effects as it goes on, but the first sixty pages were as realistic as I could make it.

But I wanted the tone to be my anchor. When Cora sees a skyscraper I didn't want her to think, What's that huge building, what do you call that? That's boring, and not what the book is about. I was trying to rein myself in and tell a story.

MC: The book is not only the story of American slavery but of how slavery impacted the story of American capitalism. You write about stolen bodies working stolen land. Why is this an important question for you to write about?

CW: I was raised on the counterculture movies of the seventies, where there's a strong critique of power structure. And the through-line is that you follow the money, and that's how the world works. I think you could call it Marxism, but I believe that it's always about money, in the end.

And everyone is enslaved by a system. Cora as a girl entering puberty is expected to pump out children because more children mean more hands to work the land, means more cotton, and more cotton means more money and more slaves to sell. So she is a vessel of capitalism.

Everyone is shackled in different ways to the system, and I wanted to explore that as well.

MC: There's this question of "What is freedom?" How do we know that we possess it? Is it around the corner, or is it right here? What does it mean to be free?

CW: Sticking with Cora's point of view, she has a vision of northern slaves who have "nice" jobs. But as she travels her idea of freedom doesn't get larger, it shrinks. Hopefully I'm making enough situations in the book that she can test her ideas about the world and be tested in her own right.

MC: This novel makes me think, you know, in the midst of the Black Lives Matter movement, and in the midst of a hellish presidential campaign, this book deeply troubles any notions—especially white liberal notions—of historical progress in the field of race relations. Do you feel that we've made progress in race relations since the time of slavery? What does racial progress mean to you?

CW: It's so incremental. Talking about the book and what I learned about slavery in elementary school, you know, one day we did a section on slavery and Lincoln, and Lincoln comes and frees the slaves. And that's all we talked about. Then a couple of years later, maybe there was something about "separate but equal." And then Martin Luther King comes, and everything is fine.

Who wants to think about how their great-great-grandfather raped and brutalized a bunch of other human beings? Who wants to think about how your great-great-grandfather or grandmother was brutalized? It's hard to tackle in your mind.

I think there's a notion of hope in the book, and while Cora does endure many tribulations, I think she comes to a place that is pretty far from where she started.

The Carnegie Interview:
Colson Whitehead

Donna Seaman / 2016

From *Booklist*, December 16, 2016. © 2016 The Booklist Reader (part of the American Library Association). Reprinted with permission.

Donna Seaman: I want to begin with the novel's literal underground railroad, which has actual tunnels, tracks, trains, and stations. This imaginative approach reminded me of the elevators in your first novel, *The Intuitionist*, and, in *John Henry Days*, the contest between man and machine. I wonder if these earlier riffs on humans and technology inspired aspects of this novel.

Colson Whitehead: With those two books, I started from a weird question or premise—what if an elevator inspector had to solve a criminal case? Or what if we updated this industrial-age anxiety myth of John Henry for the information age?

In my early books, I started with what-if stories, then with *Sag Harbor*, I started thinking about character and situation more. The what-if-ness aspect of *The Underground Railroad* goes back to the earlier books, but it weds an oddball premise with a really strong foundation in characters. I think it marries two different strands of my work.

And I do skip over how this underground railroad actually works. I'm not so interested in explaining it; it's really more like a doorway allowing Cora to get from state to state and episode to episode.

DS: I was struck by how very tactile everything is in your novel, so tangible, so intimate. How did you achieve that?

CW: I think by just doing the research, especially reading the voices of former slaves in the slave narratives or oral histories collected by the federal government's Works Progress Administration in the 1930s, by sticking true to how people described their own experiences being brutalized under the slave system, especially the matter-of-factness found in many of these accounts, I had a voice for the narrator in my novel that is rooted in the details, the brutal particulars.

DS: Was Cora, your protagonist, an amalgam of the voices you were reading?

CW: I think she comes from trying to figure out the personality of someone who makes that imaginative step off the plantation. Out of all the millions, there was only a fraction of people able to conceive of running because, obviously, the stakes were so high and the punishment was so great if you were captured. What kind of person conceives of running away like that?

DS: What about Caesar? He's also a very compelling character, and he offers a different view of the situation.

CW: Caesar is someone who knows how to read, who grew up in the North and is transported to the southern system. He's another representative of plantation life. Other characters—Sam, who helps Cora in South Carolina, versus Martin in North Carolina—represent different kinds of people who are reluctant or enthusiastic supporters of the railroad.

The way I see it, this book is being rebooted every sixty pages as we get to each new state along the railroad, which allowed me to have a really big cast . . . This approach made it possible for me to have a much bigger path than a more realistic novel would allow. It gave me a way to explore different perspectives on free men, a different way to look at white abolitionists and slave masters. The structure allowed me to have a lot of different voices in the book.

DS: As fantastic as many elements of the novel are, it is also a very traditional odyssey, albeit with the added twist of having your hero emerge from the underground in one surprising place after another.

CW: The structure is definitely old. The protagonist is on a journey through different episodes that have allegorical flourishes, and she's being tested at one after another as she tries to find that final port of home, a safe place of refuge. It allowed me to take her to a lot of different places.

For me, each new section was very exciting to get to because I'm allowed to have these different schemes and arenas for Cora to battle against and be tested. Whenever she popped out of the underground, I was very excited to create a new land for sixty pages before I changed it again.

DS: It really gives readers a vivid sense of the vastness and complexity of the divided nation. It's interesting, too, that Cora reflects on the very idea of freedom; she says freedom is a thing that shifted as you looked at it. That perception underlines what she finds in each place, especially when appearances are deceiving. At one point, she ends up as part of an exhibit in the Museum of Living History. There really were such displays at world fairs and exhibitions, where Native Americans and Africans enacted scenes. Was this a source of inspiration?

CW: Oh yeah. World's fairs, exhibitions, carnivals—P. T. Barnum would display African Americans in jungle garb and have them portray African stereotypes. There's a lot of stuff that seems absurd when you first encounter it in the book, but it's all rooted in something that actually happened. The Museum of Living History episode is not very embroidered. What Cora goes through in that section is far tamer than the disgusting extremes of actual world's fairs and carnivals.

DS: We were talking about how your earlier books can be seen as stepping stones to *The Underground Railroad*. What about *Zone One*, your zombie novel?

CW: The way I see it, one of the backbones of postapocalypse literature is the search for a safe refuge, whether in postnuclear war fiction or zombie novels. People are always looking for that human refuge over the next hill. Then they find a place, it's overrun, and they have to keep going. They're animated by a very improbable hope that they can be safe. I think that is what animates Mark Spitz in *Zone One* and a lot of heroes in postapocalypse literature. I think that impossible hope also animates Cora. Why should she believe that there is any place of freedom when all she's witnessed her whole life is the brutality of the plantation? Yet she persists.

DS: Cora describes America as her warden, which suggests that everyone in the country, North or South, free or enslaved, was imprisoned in some way by slavery.

CW: There's a moment when Ridgeway, a runaway slave-catcher, is talking to his father, the blacksmith, whose business takes off as the cotton industry booms because he's making the chains and the nails and the wheel rims that keep the system going. Meanwhile Ridgeway is keeping the slaves in order and capturing them and bringing them back to the masters, upholding the system that way. Anyone who's financially implicated in slavery is enslaved by it.

DS: We talked earlier about Caesar, who, unlike most enslaved people, was able to learn to read. It there a connection between literacy and freedom?

CW: Becoming literate is a big part of the early slave narratives. It was actually against the law for slaves to read. Slaves were beaten if they were caught, and the owners were beaten, too. Once they got off the plantation and were free from the constraints of slavery, they could read so that moment of liberation is very important to a lot of slaves—and, of course, people in general.

DS: Reading is still an important aspect of staying free, as is access to libraries.

CW: Yes, absolutely. It's been delightful to find that out. Because I play with history, because I combine fact and faction, the true and the fake, readers have done research on their own to try to figure out how the novel works and how it's constructed, learning, along the way, more about these brief excursions I make into American history.

Additional Resources

Uncollected Writing

"Better Than Renting Out a Windowless Room: The Blessed Distraction of Technology."
   Publishers Weekly 258.17 (25 Apr. 2011): 140.
"Don't You Be My Neighbor." *New York* 37.15 (3 May 2004): 32–33.
"Down in Front." *Granta* 86 (Summer 2004): 237–42.
"The End of the Affair." *New York Times Book Review* 151 (3 Mar. 2002): 8.
"Finally, a Thin President." *New York Times* (6 Nov. 2008): 33.
"Flava of the Month." *New York* 41.15 (28 Apr. 2008): 68–70.
"The Gangsters." *New Yorker* 84.42 (22 Dec. 2008): 90–103.
"The Great Reboot." *Harper's Magazine* 318 (Jun. 2009): 38–39.
"Hard Times in the Uncanny Valley." *Grantland.com*. 24 Aug. 2012. Web. 30 May 2013,
   http: //www.grantland.com/story/_/id/8300060/colson-whitehead-olympics.
"How to Write." *New York Times Book Review* (29 Jul. 2012): 8.
"I Scream." *New York Times Magazine* 155 (16 Jul. 2006): 57–58.
"I Write in Brooklyn. Get Over It." *New York Times Book Review* (2 Mar. 2008): 31.
"Life without Pity." *New York Times Magazine* 164 (8 Mar. 2015): 17–19.
"Lost and Found." *New York Times Magazine* 151 (11 Nov. 2001): 23–25.
"Note to Self." *New York Times Magazine* 164 (5 Apr. 2015): 13.
"Occasional Dispatches from the Republic of Anhedonia." *Grantland.com*. 10 Jul. 2011.
   30 May 2013, http: //www.grantland.com/story/_/id/6754551/.
"Operators Are Standing By." *New York Times* (16 Mar. 2014): BR10.
"Picking a Genre." *New York Times Book Review* (1 Nov. 2009): 23.
"A Psychotronic Childhood." *New Yorker* 88.16 (4 Jun. 2012): 98–105.
"Swept Away." *New York Times Magazine* 152 (3 Nov. 2002): 15–16.
"Visible Man." *New York Times* (24 Apr. 2008): 25.
"What We Don't See." *New York Times Magazine* 164 (31 May 2015): 13–15.
"When Spirits Linger." Review of *Lincoln in the Bardo* by George Saunders. *New York
   Times* (12 Feb. 2017): BR1.
"When Zombies Attack!" (with Alex Pappademas) *Grantland.com*. 7 Oct 2011. Web. 30
   May 2013, http: //www.grantland.com/story/_/id/7113150/when-zombies-attack.
"Wow, Fiction Works!" *Harper's Magazine* 318 (Feb. 2009): 29–31.
"The Year of Living Postracially." *New York Times* (4 Nov. 2009): 31.

Scholarly Books on Whitehead's Work

Fain, Kimberly. *Colson Whitehead: The Postracial Voice of Contemporary Literature.* Lanham, MD: Rowman & Littlefield, 2015.
Maus, Derek C. *Understanding Colson Whitehead.* Columbia: University of South Carolina Press, 2014.

Scholarly Articles on Whitehead's Work

Berlant, Lauren. "Intuitionists: History and the Affective Event." *American Literary History* 20.4 (Winter 2008): 845–60.
Bérubé, Michael. "Race and Modernity in Colson Whitehead's *The Intuitionist.*" *The Holodeck in the Garden: Science and Technology in Contemporary American Fiction.* Ed. Peter Freese and Charles B. Harris. Normal, IL: Dalkey Archive Press, 2004. 163–78.
Brown, Stephanie. "Conclusion: 'Horizontal Thinking in a Vertical World Is the Race's Curse,' or 'Is This a Raced Novel, or a Novel That Happens to Be about Race?': A Note on Teaching Colson Whitehead's *The Intuitionist.*" In *Engaging Tradition, Making It New: Essays on Teaching Recent African American Literature.* Eds. Stephanie Brown and Éva Tettenborn. Newcastle: Cambridge Scholars, 2008. 143–53.
Butler, Robert. "The Postmodern City in Colson Whitehead's *The Colossus of New York* and Jeffrey Renard Allen's *Rails under My Back.*" *CLA Journal* 48.1 (Sep. 2004): 71–87.
Caughey, John S. "'A Zombie Novel with Brains': Bringing Genre to Life in the Classroom." *Teaching American Literature: A Journal of Theory and Practice* 7.3–4 (Fall–Winter 2015): 1–22.
Cohn, Jesse S. "Odd Afflictions: Colson Whitehead's *Apex Hides the Hurt* and the 'Post-Soul Condition.'" *The Journal of the Midwest Modern Language Association* 42.1 (Spring 2009): 15–24.
Collins, Peter. "The Ghosts of Economics Past: *John Henry Days* and the Production of History." *African American Review* 46.2/3 (Summer/Fall 2013): 285–300.
Cvek, Sven. "Surviving Utopia in *Zone One.*" In *Facing the Crises: Anglophone Literature in the Postmodern World.* Ed. Ljubica Matek and Jasna Poljak Rehlicki. Newcastle-upon-Tyne: Cambridge Scholars, 2014. 2–14.
Dallmann, Antje. "ConspiraCities and Creative Paranoia: Ellis's *Glamorama*, Hustvedt's *The Blindfold*, and Whitehead's *The Intuitionist.*" *Anglophonia: French Journal of English Studies* 19 (2006): 67–78.
De Caro, Frank. "'Authentic Local Culture': *John Henry Days* and the Open Textuality of a Folk Tradition." *The Folklore Historian* 23 (2006): 3–18.
Elam, Michele. "Passing in the Post-Race Era: Danzy Senna, Philip Roth, and Colson Whitehead." *African American Review* 41.4 (Winter 2007): 749–68. [Discusses *The Intuitionist*]
Forsberg, Soren. "'Don't Believe Your Eyes.'" *Transition: An International Review* 109 (2012): 130–43. [Discusses *Zone One*]
Gauthier, Tim S. "Zombies, the Uncanny, and the City: Colson Whitehead's *Zone One.*" In *The City Since 9/11: Literature, Film, Television.* Ed. Keith Wilhite. Madison, NJ: Fairleigh Dickinson University Press, 2016. 109–25.

Grattan, Sean. "I Think We're Alone Now: Solitude and the Utopian Subject in Colson Whitehead's *The Intuitionist*." *Cultural Critique* 96 (Spring 2017): 126–53.

Grausam, Daniel. "After the Post(al)." *American Literary History* 23.3 (Fall 2011): 625–42. [Discusses *John Henry Days*]

Hess, John Joseph. "Music Consumption and the Remix of Self in Colson Whitehead's *Sag Harbor*." In *Write in Tune: Contemporary Music in Fiction*. Ed. Erich Hertz and Jeffrey Roessner. London: Bloomsbury, 2014. 169–81.

Hock, Stephen. "The Black Box of Genre in Colson Whitehead's *The Intuitionist* and Charles Yu's *How to Live Safely in a Science Fictional Universe*." In *The Poetics of Genre in the Contemporary Novel*. Ed. Tim Lanzendörfer. Lanham, MD: Lexington, 2016. 57–71.

Hurley, Jessica. "History Is What Bites: Zombies, Race, and the Limits of Biopower in Colson Whitehead's *Zone One*." *Extrapolation: A Journal of Science Fiction and Fantasy* 56.3 (Fall 2015): 311–33.

Inscoe, John C. "Race and Remembrance in West Virginia: John Henry for a Post-Modern Age." *Journal of Appalachian Studies* 10.1/2 (Spring/Fall 2004): 85–94.

Katz, Tamar. "City Memory, City History: Urban Nostalgia, *The Colossus of New York*, and Late-Twentieth-Century Historical Fiction." *Contemporary Literature* 51.4 (Winter 2010): 810–51.

Kelly, Adam. "The New Sincerity." In *Postmodern/Postwar—and After: Rethinking American Literature*. Ed. Jason Gladstone, Andrew Hoberek, and Daniel Worden. Iowa City: University of Iowa Press, 2016. 197-208. [Discusses *Apex Hides the Hurt*]

Knight, Nadine M. "'It's a New Day': *The Intuitionist*, *The Wire*, and Prophetic Tradition." *MELUS: The Journal of the Society for the Study of the Multi-Ethnic Literature of the United States* 40.4 (Winter 2015): 28–44.

LaForge, Jane Rosenberg. "Colson Whitehead: The Final Frontier." *Paradoxa: Studies in World Literary Genres* 20 (2006): 129–50.

Lavender, Isiah, III. "Ethnoscapes: Environment and Language in Ishmael Reed's *Mumbo Jumbo*, Colson Whitehead's *The Intuitionist*, and Samuel R. Delany's *Babel-17*." *Science Fiction Studies* 34 (2007): 187–200.

Leader-Picone, Cameron. "Post-Black Stories: Colson Whitehead's *Sag Harbor* and Racial Individualism." *Contemporary Literature* 56.3 (Fall 2015): 421–49.

Leise, Christopher. "With Names, No Coincidence: Colson Whitehead's Postracial Puritan Allegory." *African American Review* 47.2–3 (Summer/Fall 2014): 285–300.

Lenz, Wylie. "Toward a Genealogy of the American Zombie Novel: From Jack London to Colson Whitehead." In *The Written Dead: Essays on the Literary Zombie*. Ed. Kyle William Bishop and Angela Tenga. Jefferson, NC: McFarland, 2017. 98–119.

Levine, Andrea. "'In His Own Home': Gendering the African American Domestic Sphere in Contemporary Culture." *WSQ: Women's Studies Quarterly* 39.1/2 (Spring/Summer 2011): 170–87. [Discusses *Sag Harbor*]

Li, Stephanie. "'Sometimes Things Disappear': Absence and Mutability in Colson Whitehead's *The Colossus of New York*." *Literature after 9/11*. Eds. Ann Keniston and Jeanne Follansbee Quinn. New York: Routledge, 2008. 82–98.

Libretti, Tim. "'Verticality Is Such a Risky Enterprise': Class Epistemologies and the Critique of Upward Mobility in Colson Whitehead's *The Intuitionist*." In *Class and Culture in Crime Fiction: Essays on Works in English Since the 1970s*. Ed. Julie H. Kim. Jefferson, NC: McFarland, 2014. 201–24.

Lieber, Marlon. "'It's Always Mississippi in the Fifties': Colson Whitehead's Imaginative Geography of the U.S. South." In *The South from Elsewhere*. Ed. Marcel Arbeit. Olomouc, Czech Republic: Palacký University, 2014. 115–28.

Liggins, Saundra. "The Urban Gothic Vision of Colson Whitehead's *The Intuitionist*." *African American Review* 40.2 (Summer 2006): 359–69.

Lukin, Josh. "The Resistant Body: Disability, History, and Classical Heroism in Colson Whitehead's *Apex Hides the Hurt*." In *Engaging Tradition, Making It New: Essays on Teaching Recent African American Literature*. Eds. Stephanie Brown and Éva Tettenborn. Newcastle: Cambridge Scholars, 2008. 123–42.

Marshall, Kate. "What Are the Novels of the Anthropocene? American Fiction in Geological Time." *American Literary History* 27.3 (Fall 2015): 523–38. [Discusses *Zone One*]

Ramsey, William. "An End of Southern History: The Down-Home Quests of Toni Morrison and Colson Whitehead." *African American Review* 41.4 (2007): 769–85. [Discusses *John Henry Days*]

Russell, Allison. "Recalibrating the Past: Colson Whitehead's *The Intuitionist*." *Critique* 49.1 (Fall 2007): 46–60.

Saldívar, Ramón. "The Second Elevation of the Novel: Race, Form, and the Postrace Aesthetic in Contemporary Narrative." *Narrative* 21.1 (Jan. 2013): 1–18. [Discusses *The Intuitionist*]

Schur, Richard. "The Crisis of Authenticity in Contemporary African American Literature." In *Contemporary African American Literature: The Living Canon*. Ed. Lovalerie King, Shirley Moody-Turner, Mat Johnson, and Alice Randall. Bloomington: Indiana University Press, 2013. 235–54. [Discusses *Sag Harbor*]

Selzer, Linda. "Instruments More Perfect than Bodies: Romancing Uplift in Colson Whitehead's *The Intuitionist*." *African American Review* 43.4 (Winter 2009): 681–98.

Shermeyer, Kelli. "'Systems Die Hard': Resistance and Reanimation in Colson Whitehead's *Zone One*." In *The Written Dead: Essays on the Literary Zombie*. Ed. Kyle William Bishop and Angela Tenga. Jefferson, NC: McFarland, 2017. 120–132.

Shrivastava, Jaya. "Recollection and Self-Assessment in Colson Whitehead's *John Henry Days*." *ANQ: A Quarterly Journal of Short Articles, Notes, and Reviews* 30.1 (Jan.–Mar. 2017): 58–62.

Shrivastava, Jaya, and Joe Varghese. "'The City Knows You': Spatial Consciousness in Colson Whitehead's *The Colossus of New York* (2003)." *Notes on Contemporary Literature* 43.5 (Nov. 2013): 4–6.

Sorensen, Leif. "Against the Post-Apocalyptic: Narrative Closure in Colson Whitehead's *Zone One*." *Contemporary Literature* 55.3 (Sep. 2014): 559–92.

Spencer, Rochelle. "Afro-Surreal and Afro-Futuristic Visual Technologies in Junot Díaz's *The Brief Wondrous Life of Oscar Wao* and Colson Whitehead's *Zone One*." *Pivot: A Journal of Interdisciplinary Studies and Thought* 5.1 (2016): 209–24.

Swanson, Carl Joseph. "'The Only Metaphor Left': Colson Whitehead's *Zone One* and Zombie Narrative Form." *Genre: Forms of Discourse and Culture* 47.3 (Fall 2014): 379–405.

Tettenborn, Éva. "A Mountain Full of Ghosts": Mourning African American Masculinities in Colson Whitehead's *John Henry Days*." *African American Review* 46.2/3 (Summer/Fall 2013): 271–84.

Tucker, Jeffrey Allen. "'Verticality Is Such a Risky Enterprise': The Literary and Paraliterary Antecedents of Colson Whitehead's *The Intuitionist*." *Novel: A Forum on Fiction* 43.1 (2010): 148–56.

Walonen, Michael K. "'This Making of Truth Is Violence Too, Out of Which Facts Are Formed': Colson Whitehead's Secret History of Post-Reconstruction America in *John Henry Days*." *Literature & History* 23.2 (Autumn 2014): 67–80.

Windle, Amanda. "Automation and Design for Prevention: Fictional Accounts of Misanthropic Agency from the Elevator (Lift) to the Sexbot (Chatbot)." *Technoetic Arts: A Journal of Speculative Research* 12.1 (Mar. 2014): 91–106. [Discusses *The Intuitionist*]

Wixon, Christopher. "Vertical Bearings: Dashiell Hammett's *The Maltese Falcon* and Colson Whitehead's *The Intuitionist*." *Notes on Contemporary Literature* 42.3 (May 2012): n.p.

Index

9 781496 821522